The Practice *of* Prayer

A COMPANION GUIDE

Robert Warren

A Hamewith Book

BakerBooks
A Division of Baker Book House Co
Grand Rapids, Michigan 49516

Published by Hamewith Books
an imprint of Baker Book House Company
P.O. Box 6287, Grand Rapids, MI 49516-6287

First published under the title *An Affair of the Heart* in 1994 by Highland Books, 2 High Pines, Knoll Road, Godalming, Surrey, GU7 2EP.

Printed in the United States of America

Library of Congress Cataloging-in-Publication Data

Warren, Robert, 1939–
[Affair of the heart]
The practice of prayer : a companion guide / Robert Warren.
p. cm.
Originally published: An affair of the heart. Godalming, Surrey : Highland Books, 1994.
ISBN 0-8010-6382-5 (paper)
1. Prayer. I. Title.

BV215 .W364 2001
248.3′2—dc21 2001037363

For current information about all releases from Baker Book House, visit our web site:
http://www.bakerbooks.com

Contents

Index of Prayer Principles

Index of Prayers of the Heart

List of Prayer Exercises

Introduction

The prayers of the saints are affairs of the heart.

—David Adam, *The Cry of the Deer*[1]

Christianity is about knowing God, and central to that knowing is the practice of prayer. Few who seek to follow Christ would disagree with that. The difficulty comes in putting it into practice.

During the past several years, I have traveled around the country seeking to help individuals and churches "make Christ known" not just by what they say, but also by who they are, by what they do, and by how they are church. Time and time again it has struck me that life, in individual believers and in local church communities, is directly proportional to the reality of people's engagement with God.

Church as organized religion, with its meetings, programs, and various ways of joining in and signing up, is not the first port of call for many today. Yet, plenty of people are looking for spirituality, and that is likely to be the main door through which people enter the faith today.

Spirituality is one of today's "in" words. Although dangerously slippery as a term, with a vast range of definitions to suit all tastes, it yet expresses some very important things happening in the world at present. It signals a thirst engendered by our cultural addiction to material possessions. They simply cannot deliver the goods when it comes to a sense of meaning, purpose, and the capacity to enjoy life to the full. Add to that the strong doses of suspicion and daily diet of cynicism, and it is hardly surprising that such a thirst exists. We long for life to make sense, to have meaning, to add up to something. The current interest in spirituality points to the widespread desire to find some way of living which expresses that there is more to life than an upturn in the economy or some escapist experience.

So our churches need to become centers of spiritual life and vitality. I have seen and known, both in personal experience and as a vicar in one parish for over twenty years, that

> We cannot evangelize until we have been evangelized. This happens most powerfully through solitary prayer.
>
> —John Michael Talbot[2]

I know of no better way to help Christians *share* their faith than to help them *exercise* that faith through prayer so that they have a story to tell.

Context

It is important to set prayer in the context of today's culture, for if we do not understand our setting in history we are unlikely to break through to authentic prayer. We need to start by considering some of the ways in which modern culture makes prayer more difficult.

The pace of life is prayer-resistant. When I was the Team Rector of a flourishing church, I used to wonder out loud whether the attractiveness of the church was, at least in part, because it was "a frantic church in a frantic society." Newcomers felt at home! We need to find some way to become "a still church in a frantic society." Prayer and stillness are certainly close cousins, but they have not been seeing much of each other recently.

Our way of communicating is prayer-resistant. We live in a culture that has been deeply shaped by rational, scientific thinking and by cerebral, verbal communication. We tend to restrict prayer to "words said"—but prayer is much richer than that. As C. S. Lewis says:

> I still think the prayer without words is the best—if one can really achieve it.
>
> —C. S. Lewis[3]

However, today's culture is changing rapidly, from a word-conscious to an image-conscious one. Sound bites and photo opportunities now largely shape political communication, as the use of images largely shapes advertising. Advertisements tell us little about the product but transport us into an idyllic setting that's meant to leave an association with the wonders of the car/perfume/chocolate/toilet bowl cleaner being promoted.

My intention in what follows is to open up some of these other, and arguably richer, avenues of prayer than the purely verbal. We have much to learn from the church, down the whole history of Christendom, which could well help us make connection with God in the new culture into which we are moving.

Our way of reading is prayer-resistant. The way we think and communicate in our culture means that we easily end up reading Scripture like the handbook for operating a microwave oven, in a literal, mechanical way. If you read the Psalms or parables of Jesus like that they will seem dull indeed, and of little or no aid to engaging in prayer. Reading Scripture is much more than finding out the facts.

Moreover, such a way of seeing reality misses out on the great areas of prayer that have enriched Christian prayer for two millennia—symbols, stories, rituals, and a sense of awe and wonder. By exploring them, I hope also to help liberate us a little from the constraints on the whole of life imposed by the narrowness of our Western way of seeing and living life.

If, in the process of growing in our experience and expression of prayer, we could break through some of these constraints, it might have a significant effect on the work of evangelism. For we would be evangelizing our way of seeing life and reality. It was the medieval mystics who said that evangelism is sharing the fruits of our contemplation with others. Much of the teaching of Jesus seems to have that source, for he was sharing the fruit of his meditation on Scripture ("You have heard it said . . .") and on the world around him (hence, the parables).

Not So Much a Book, More a Way of Doing Prayer

Interesting and often helpful though books about prayer are, this book is focused specifically on helping in the *practice* of prayer. It is more of a prayer manual than a discussion about prayer. It arises out of my conviction that much of the seeming impotence of the church in the West can be traced back to the lack of reality in our engaging with God at the personal level. Talking *about* is no substitute for talking *to* God.

It is for this reason that the book contains several ingredients. First, there is the actual *text* of the book itself in which I spell out various aspects of prayer. Second, in each chapter (except Chapter Twelve) there is a *prayer exercise* that relates to the material of the chapter. It is intended to be used repeatedly until it becomes part of our way of praying. (More about that in a moment.) Third, a series of *prayer principles* is scattered throughout the book; they are appropriately highlighted in the text. If we can get hold of, and learn to practice them, these principles will lay a foundation on which a stronger prayer life can be built. Fourth, scattered through the book are a number of *prayers of the heart.* These are prayers that express some major aspect of the life of prayer, and which are best learned by heart. They will then arise out of our inner being wherever we are, including times of sickness or when our eyesight or other faculties have failed, to enrich our closing years of discipleship. These various aspects are all part of the goal of going beyond this being another book about prayer, into being a book that is prayer-productive. The aim is to stimulate and guide the practice of prayer.

I conclude this introduction with some suggestions about how to make the most of what follows.

Practice

My encouragement is to *pray along with this book* and not just to read it. While it may be worth reading through the book first to get the overall feel and direction, its primary value will be in assisting the work and practice of praying.

Here there is a paradox at the heart of learning to pray. While we can learn much from various schools of prayer and spiritual directors, it is also true that the only way you can pray is the way that *you* can pray. Prayer is unique to each individual. I have no desire, therefore, to impose a foreign way of praying on others. Yet, each of us can benefit from being stretched to pray beyond the confines of our present patterns. The long-term purpose of being stretched to pray in new ways is that they will become natural to *our* way of praying. So all that is presented here needs to be integrated into the way of praying that is authentic to each individual.

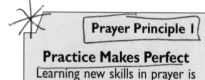

> **Prayer Principle 1**
>
> **Practice Makes Perfect**
>
> Learning new skills in prayer is always initially self-conscious. We have to press through this stage to reach the productive stage beyond.

Developing our prayer life is like learning to drive a car. Initially it is all so slow and self-conscious. Is the seat in the right place? Can I see out of the mirrors? Where does the ignition key go? Is the car in gear? Where is the emergency brake, and is it on? All these questions crowd into the mind of the learner—even before the car is turned on. Experienced drivers are well on their way before they have given much conscious thought to the work of driving. They have assimilated the practice into unconscious skills.

Accept that learning new skills in prayer is always self-conscious—but only in the learning stage. My encouragement is to press on through the seeming artificiality of new skills to the place where we have assimilated them and find them enriching our practice of prayer. C. S. Lewis says:[4]

> As long as you notice, and have to count, the steps, you are not yet dancing but only learning to dance.

The important point is not to be put off by self-consciousness, but to press on through it to the place where "it works" and "I can do it" describe your experience. Without this willingness to press on through the newness, we will not develop new skills.

Like learning to drive a car, or dance, it is best to *tackle one aspect at a time.* My encouragement to those wanting to stretch their prayer muscles is to work on one thing at a time. It may be listening prayer, or beholding the throne, or practicing the presence of God that we feel the desire or need to develop. Read the relevant chapter, do the exercise provided, and stay with that for a month or more. As you do you will assimilate new skills and incorporate them into your own prayer life. The more you practice, the more you will find *your* way of praying taking shape.

Establishing a regular time of prayer or a regular time to work on the exercises in this book is an important part of preparing to pray. Allocating a manageable amount and frequency of prayer is much better than laying unrealistic and discouraging expectations on ourselves. Better to decide on three sessions of ten minutes of actual prayer per week, and achieve that, than attempt an hour a day and fail miserably. Once you have achieved your target you can stretch it.

If you are committing yourself to prayer, and working through this book, then it is more a matter of committing yourself to twenty minutes to read a chapter and ten minutes to do the prayer exercise at the end, once a week, and then to repeat the exercise for the next few days/weeks until you are familiar with it and have incorporated it into your prayer life.

If you start with the book and the exercises, do not be put off by feelings of self-consciousness and artificiality. As time, and you, progress, those feelings will fade and a growing sense of this way of praying being natural to you will begin, like crocuses in spring, to show themselves as signs of hope and experiences of joy.

Perhaps, this book may be of most help, if having read it through, you then use the prayer principles scattered through the text as an aid to the strengthening of your prayer life. You are likely to find that a number have already been established. Simply by seeing them in the specific terms in which they are set out can strengthen your already existing practice of them.

Developing Your Own Prayer Book

Keeping a journal is a helpful way to grow in prayer. (There is more about the practice of doing this in the Postscript.) Use it to record prayers that arise out of your growth in prayer. You can put quotations, pictures, and prayers down for future and repeated reference. Most important, you can record the story of your journey in prayer. The important thing is to tell it the way it is. Looking over it from time to time will help you to understand the journey you have made so far, and so give understanding of what the next steps need to be.

I also find it a great help to record the prayers (of others, and those that arise spontaneously out of my own experience) that particularly resonate with my experience of life.

That word *resonate* has a historical context for me. I was officiating at a wedding in a church with eight chancel steps. I was at the top of them, the bride and groom were one step below, and, as I took the ring from the best man, I noticed that there was a register running along the base of the bottom step. The moment of fear ("will I drop the ring?") was followed by a matching action—I dropped it! "Ping, ping, ping" it went as it hit the top step and bounced up again three times. Suddenly out of my subconscious leapt the awareness that I used to be a good goalee at school—especially when the ball was low. In an instant I bent my knees, scooped the ring up at ankle height, and recovered the ring.

However, I knew that everybody was aware of what had happened. The ping of that tiny ring had resonated around the whole church. It might have been Big Ben striking for all the attention it drew to itself. It is etched deeply into my understanding of the fact that "to resonate" means "to give characteristic vibrations in sympathy with another body." It has become an important word for me in prayer. There are some prayers that "fill with vibrations" and find a deep echo with me. Those are the prayers I record, and use again and again. They attune me to the presence of the Divine.

The Spiritual Exercises of Robert Warren

I have to admit that the phrase heading this section does not have quite the ring of the phrase from which it is taken, namely, *The Spiritual Exercises of Ignatius of Loyola!* However, I dare to use the phrase because this book really is a book of spiritual or prayer exercises, and I find the whole idea of exercise fits well with my understanding and experience of prayer.

We take exercise, or do exercises, for our own health and well-being. So too with prayer. Exercise demands effort, but the experts tell us not to overstretch ourselves. So too with prayer. We have to learn new exercises and then we can become proficient in their practice and grow in what we can do through them. So too with prayer. A regular ten or so minutes is much better than a marathon every decade. So too with prayer.

In particular, a schedule of exercises is designed to use, develop, and bring to fitness our whole body. So there will be neck and shoulder exercises, upper body exercises, chest exercises, leg and arm exercises, and so on. So too with prayer. This is a major part of this book. The different parts of the body, as far as prayer is concerned, include the use of the body itself (how we sit and how we breathe), the use of the eyes (with the use of pictures of places and people that have "spoken to us" and of icons), the use of our imagination (either in reading Scripture or in a prayer visitation, or of a trouble-spot in the news), and the development of our capacity for wonder, awe, and stillness. The aim of this book is to help us develop our prayer muscles. It is a form of spiritual aerobics, although definitely not narrowly spiritual since an important concern is to connect the inner spiritual life with our outer experience of reality.

On Fire

Your picking up and reading this book is an indication of your desire to grow in the glorious skill and gift of prayer. My prayer is that those who see it through to the end may find it to be an enriching experience that is life-giving not just to our prayer life, but rather to the whole of life. As Jesus so clearly demonstrated, to pray is to live and to grow in prayer is to grow in the capacity to enjoy life.

Prayer of the Heart

Caim for stilling our hearts
(a "caim" is a Celtic "circle prayer")

Encircle me, O God,
keep faith within,
keep pride without.

Encircle me, O God,
keep hope within,
keep despair out.

Encircle me, O God,
keep love within,
keep fear without.

—Adapted from David Adam's
The Cry of the Deer, pp. 11ff.

Roberta Bondi, in her fine book *To Pray and to Love (Conversations on Prayer with the Desert Fathers),* quotes this wonderful story from one of the desert fathers:

> Abba Lot went to see Abba Joseph and said to him, "Abba, as far as I can, I say my little office, I fast a little, I pray and meditate, I live in peace and as far as I can, I purify my thoughts. What else can I do?" Then the old man stood up and stretched his hands toward heaven. His fingers became like ten lamps of fire and he said to him, "If you will, you can become all flame."

Prayer Exercise: In Company with the Three Graces

- Sit down, still yourself from the busyness around you, from which you have come, and relax your limbs.
- Repeat the following two lines *(from the hymn "Come, Holy Spirit, ever One,"* which can be found on p. 46 of *Celebrating Common Prayer):*

  Love light up our mortal frame,
  Till others catch the living flame.

- Say it half a dozen to a dozen times, until you no longer have to look at the words on the page. Slow down the pace each time you repeat it, until the saying of it itself is part of the relaxing process.
- Then say it "in the company of the three graces" (faith, hope, and love), repeating it in the awareness of each of these graces in turn.
  - *Say it with faith* (repeating it several times), looking to God and expecting him to bring fulfillment of this godly desire to birth in your life.
  - *Say it with hope,* looking to what your prayer life can become. Let hope open your eyes to the sort of person you can be as the result of being shaped by prayer. See the words of this prayer coming to life in your life. See yourself enlarged in your openness to the whole of life, and

more comfortable with living as a creature before the Creator, ignited by love of God and love from God.

- *Say it with love,* receiving love as a gift—not straining after it as achievement or making it "another thing I ought to do." Know that through prayer you are connected to the source of love. Do not depend on feelings. They come and go. God's love abides, beneath the changing waters of life, his depths are underneath the often choppy seas of life.

Part 1

ENCOUNTER

Chapter 1

On the Threshold

Clearing the Obstacles to Prayer

> I am a firm believer in regular devotions. In fact I study my Bible almost every day of the week. Almost on Monday, almost on Tuesday, almost on . . .
>
> —Church of England newspaper cartoon

Our half-Siamese black cat—whose mother had a long pedigree but no morals, and whose father was never seen again—is put out each evening. My locking-up routine involves letting him back in. Frequently, when I open the front door, I find him sitting on the mat outside. He has developed a range of responses. Sometimes he continues to look straight ahead without even an acknowledgment that the door has opened or that the master of the house has called. Sometimes he does look round, but not for long. On occasions I step down to pick him up, only to have him shoot away into the night not to be seen until the next morning. And, sometimes, he gets up, turns around, and walks into the house as if this were his invariable practice.

Christians are like that when it comes to prayer. We have been invited into the presence of God ("to dwell in the house of the LORD forever," Ps. 23:6), but we often stand unsure on the threshold. We know the way is open, but we sometimes feel too unsure even to dare to notice. At other times we know prayer is an option but do not avail ourselves of this invitation. Too often, we run and hide ourselves in activity. And sometimes we are able to walk into God's presence as if this were the most natural thing in the world.

The Most Natural Thing in the World

At one level prayer is that. Opinion polls show that most people in the United Kingdom pray. The human heart is built like that. As St. Augustine put it, "Our hearts are restless until they find their rest in Thee." The Christian understanding of this human instinct is that we are made to be worshiping creatures. We all instinctively focus our living around some "center." "She lived for her family," "he lived for his work," are phrases one hears so often at funerals. It tells you where the center of a person's life is, or was.

We recognize more easily the false worship, "the idols," of those addicted to drugs or alcohol or the pursuit of money, but anything that takes the ultimate focus off God in a person's life is an idol, irrespective of whether it is a good thing like the family, or a bad thing like drugs. The point to grasp here is that all these centers are ways of worship—manifestations of the human hunger for connectedness with Ultimate Reality, for a sense of the Transcendence, for what Rudolf Otto called the "Holy Other."

This touches on the paradox of human existence. We hunger and long for relationship with God—and yet we do anything to avoid it. So, if we are to make progress in prayer, we need to see not only that it is a very natural and human response to life, but that it is also something that we instinctively avoid.

Progress will therefore involve the removal of the obstacles. For the fact is that our normal experience is that prayer is a struggle, and often leaves us feeling that, whatever our gift may be, it is not being a gifted pray-er. Why is there this strange ambivalence and uncertainty as to whether we want to pray or not? We are like the proverbial porcupines wanting to keep warm in winter but unsure as to whether the pain of closeness is not greater than the warmth generated.

Prayer of the Heart

Collect for purity

(receiving God's goodness)

Almighty God, to whom all hearts are open, all desires known, and from whom no secrets are hidden: cleanse the thoughts of our hearts by the inspiration of your Holy Spirit, that we may perfectly love you, and worthily magnify your holy name; through Christ our Lord. Amen.

—ASB, p. 119

It was Henry Ford who said that "thinking is such hard work, which is why so few people engage in it." Perhaps he had not tried prayer, which is even more demanding. Or so it seems.

Obstacles to Prayer

If we are to stand any chance of entering in through the door that has been opened for us, we are going to have to leave behind these hindrances, for they block our way in. Or rather, the blockages within us make our response to the invitation so varied and seemingly unpredictable that we struggle to make progress.

William Cowper, the hymn writer, expressed the feelings of many of us when he wrote:

> What various hindrances we meet,
> in coming to the mercy seat!
> Yet who that knows the worth of prayer
> but wishes to be often there?

Did he overstate the case? Do we wish to be "often there"? If we do, we also have to admit that our wishes are impotent. So let us look at the obstacles and see if we can clear them out of our way. There are three that stand out, in my experience and from my listening to the experience of others.

Allergy

We had better start with the most threatening obstacle—sin. It is our distance from God in character and moral judgment, in wisdom and courage, which keeps us at arm's length. We are like Adam and Eve hiding in the garden (of activity).

Our problem is compounded by poor diagnosis. All too often today, we see sin in a shallow way. Certainly if you have just sworn at your boss or spouse it makes you feel unworthy to pray. But surface actions are not the real problems. The obstacle is deeper than that. The real killers of the prayer life are pride and unbelief, for pride says, "Leave this to me, God, I can handle it," and unbelief says, "If I don't do something no one (not even God) will." Not that we say these words, even to ourselves. Yet they lie at the base of much of our attitude toward life and God. Indeed, a major part of the problem is that we deny the truth, and so cannot find healing. There is no one so difficult to cure as people who think they are fit. That is the deep-seated and corrosive nature of sin. Richard Lovelace defines sin as

> an organic network of compulsive attitudes, beliefs and behavior, deeply rooted in our alienation from God.
>
> —Richard Lovelace[1]

The problem is that deep. The Puritans were right: Mankind does have an allergy to God. The apostle Paul, in his reflections on the state of human nature, concludes that sin is essentially hatred toward God—"the sinful mind is hostile to God" (Rom. 8:7).

Irena Ratushinskaya, the Russian poet imprisoned under the communist regime simply for writing poems about God, spoke about her experience at the C. S. Lewis Oxford Institute in 1992. She said she had come to the conclusion that the former Soviet Union was not, as it claimed, an atheistic state. It was not atheistic, that is, not believing in God, but one that believed in God but was motivated by a deep hatred toward him. An anti-God crusade, she said, lay close to the heart of the orientation of the whole structure of government and education. Indeed, she said she came to faith because, with everyone and the whole system against God, she thought it was unfair and someone ought to be on his side!

One of the clearest evidences of this pride and unbelief can be seen in the way that we approach prayer. We see it as something that we do, or are quite capable of doing. We may complain that God does not always turn up, but we actually feel (although rarely admit) that not attaining success in prayer is not for lack of *our* trying.

Our allergy to God is real. The good news is that help is at hand. For the truth of the matter is that prayer is beyond us. It can only be done by the grace of God—but by the grace of God *it can be done.* That is something which God is always ready to do. The problem is at our end. Paul grasped this truth when he said, "We do not know what we ought to pray for, but the Spirit himself intercedes for us with groans that words cannot express" (Rom. 8:26). The disciples were similarly aware of their inability to pray and were provoked by the poverty of their prayer life compared with what they had seen of the prayer life of Jesus, so they dared to say, "Lord, teach us to pray" (Luke 11:1).

The first Beatitude is glorious good news about our allergy if we could but grasp it:

> Blessed are the poor in spirit, for theirs is the kingdom of heaven.
>
> —Matthew 5:3

The reason that this is such good news is that it is an invitation to us to own our weakness and look to God for help. Once we do that we have begun to engage in true prayer, which is a divinely energized way of communication between frail creature and merciful Creator. All we have to do is own the fact that prayer is not something we can do on our own. Then, in that very act we begin to pray. For grace—a sheer, undeserved gift—is the basis of prayer just as it is the basis of all creation, including the gift of life itself. And it is grace that lays the axe to the root of pride and unbelief. If we simply admit that we cannot pray, but that God—by his Spirit—can enable us to pray, then we can build a prayer life on the only sure foundation there is: God's generosity to his whole creation.

Too easily today we come to prayer as if all we needed was a little more information, and a little more effort, and the job would be done. The sober truth is that, as the Anglican Prayer Book puts it, "without You we are not able to please You."

What we need is the same attitude as that of the church in the early centuries of Christian discipleship. Then, when someone professed faith, the first thing the church did was to administer exorcism. By this act the church was dealing with the fact that "the god of this age has blinded the minds of unbelievers" (2 Cor. 4:4). So, too, we need to lay aside our pretensions to be able to pray, and then ask God for his help. It will open the door to prayer—prayer on the proper basis of a relationship with God sustained by God himself.

Frailty

Having addressed the major obstacle to our praying, namely, the deep-seated allergy to God in the human heart, we can turn now to the matter that often engages our attention: the feeling that "I don't know what to do." We feel the need for practical help. That, of course, is a great step to take for it is a recognition of our creatureliness and our need of help. It makes us open to help from others.

God alone can deal with our allergy, but the saints around us and who have gone before us can give us much help and encouragement with our frailty. However, as I have already said, you can only pray in the way that you can pray. In other words there is a unique way of praying for every believer—rather like our fingerprints, it is part of our uniqueness before God.

My intention, therefore, in all that follows, is so to draw on the resources of the "saints" so that we can make prayer our own and incorporate insights into our own way of praying. This takes time, and it is important that not too much is attempted at once. I suspect that working through the exercises (for example, one a month) until we have made them all our own will take at least two or three years. This book is really a "prayer companion," something to have alongside you where you pray so that you can dip into it for new resources for your prayer life from time to time.

Prayer is like a journey, and I neither want to lay down railroad tracks that entirely dictate the how, when, and where of that journey, nor simply describe the beautiful sunset that appears on the distant horizon but leave the reader with no help in getting there. The writers of the Book of Common Prayer expressed the same concern in the marvelous language of their day when they wrote:

> It hath been the wisdom of the Church of England, ever since the first compiling of her Publick Liturgy, to keep the mean between the two extremes, of too much stiffness in refusing, and too much easiness in admitting any variation from it.
>
> —Book of Common Prayer[2]

What follows is more like giving a map, a compass, and some basic instructions about how to make the best use of them. They are given so that you may make your journey. Or to change the metaphor, I have supplied some ingredients for the prayer life, plus a recipe, but you may have to vary the ingredients according to what is available, and the means of cooking, in order for you to make the cake that *you* are best able to make.

Folly

The third obstacle to prayer is our sheer folly. Here is the greatest gift known to humanity—the privilege of communing with the God who created us and all that is—and yet we neglect this pearl of great price, which is the gift of the gospel.

As a clergyman, I acknowledge that this is one of the great ironies of our life. We know, and spend most of our waking hours teaching others, how the heart of the good news is that each one of us can know the living God. Yet we take so little time to avail ourselves of this gift and privilege.

I had a sobering experience of this while leading a team of five clergy and one layman in my former parish. We had identified some major problem in the life of the church and, as chairman of the team, I had asked, "What shall we do about this?" All five clergyman were about to open their mouths to give the group the benefit of their insights when the layman cut the conversation short by saying, "Pray, you dumbos!" It was a timely reminder of our instinct to manage by ourselves, and only turn to God as a last resort—yet we had all preached against such attitudes. How right Rudolf Bultmann, the celebrated German theologian, was when he defined sin in these terms:

> Sin is man's determination to manage by himself.

This folly of not availing ourselves of the greatest privilege of the Christian faith is nothing new. Bernard of Clairvaux, one of the greatest leaders of the Benedictine order of monks, writing in the twelfth century, saw this same folly in his day. He expresses his dismay in his exposition of the opening words of the Song of Songs, "Let him kiss me with the kisses of his mouth." Bernard begins his commentary with these words:

> During my frequent pondering on the burning desire with which the patriarchs longed for the incarnation of Christ, I am stung by sorrow and shame. Even now I can scarcely restrain my tears, so filled with shame am I by the lukewarmness, the frigid unconcern of these miserable times. For which of us does

the consummation of that event fill with as much joy as the mere promise of it inflamed the desires of the holy men of pre-Christian times.

Preparing the Way

There is a danger in beginning a book on prayer by writing about the obstacles. Those who pick up the book looking for help might well feel discouraged and confirmed in their sense of failure. However, the reason for doing so is positive in intention. Obstacles to prayer act like a ball and chain around the ankle of the runner-after-prayer. The best way to make progress is to admit that they are there and take them off.

The work of this chapter has been like the task of the Voice in the Wilderness as recorded in Isaiah, who called:

> In the desert prepare
> the way for the LORD;
> make straight in the wilderness
> a highway for our God.
> Every valley shall be raised up,
> every mountain and hill made low;
> the rough ground shall become level,
> the rugged places a plain.
> And the glory of the LORD will be revealed,
> and all mankind together will see it.
> For the mouth of the LORD has spoken.
>
> —Isaiah 40:3–5

Our prayer life often seems like a desert and a wilderness. The promise is that right there is where God can build a way into his presence. In fact, the Voice sees the preparation as making us ready for his coming. He is the One who will "visit" us with his salvation and presence. Our task is to make "a way."

We can do that as we remove the high places—the mountains and hills. There are two that come to mind. First is the allergy that reveals the pride of our independence from God. We remove that simply by owning it and giving it to God for him to incinerate; that is what confession is. Second is the other sense in which "high places" is used in Scripture. These are places where other gods hold sway and idols are worshiped. We will look at that in more detail in Chapter Six ("Good Grief!"). However, this is the good news about repentance: Once we have the courage to own something as our responsibility we are able to give it away in confession to God. It is what we deny that "clings so closely." The allergy of pride can be named for what it is and dealt with swiftly in that way. The very act opens us up to God and his coming in grace.

Frailty and folly are more like the valleys—the gaps that need to be filled in. They are more easily dealt with. Frailty can be leveled by learning from others, folly by seeing our prayerlessness as such. Moreover, when we see answers to our frailty, in the form of some accessible "how to pray" helps, we can then step out of our folly and enter into prayer.

So now we can turn our attention to entering into prayer as we consider an overall framework that describes both how we meet God in the whole of life and how we meet him in prayer.

Prayer Exercise: Letting Go and Receiving, Before God

Sit down in a relaxed manner, resting your hands on your upper thighs, with your palms facing down.

Letting Go

- See your "hands down" as expressing a letting go of anything that blocks your awareness of God. Remember that "underneath are the everlasting arms" (Deut. 33:27 RSV).
- You are not "letting go" into a dark abyss but into the hands of the God who sustains you.
- You will often find that, at the right time, the matters you let go will pop back into your mind, complete with an answer, a solution, a way forward, or a new perspective attached.

God is creative and productive in his taking care of us. We can let go safely.

- Name your excuses for not praying.
- Feel your fears of God/prayer/failure.
- Picture your allergies, frailty, and folly.
- Let them go, imagining them dropping out of your hands, off your fingertips.

(You may find it helpful to think of them like stones dropped into a pond: you see the splash each time and you know it has gone. You may be able to feel the relief and freedom.)

Taking Hold

- Turn your hands upwards, still resting them on your thighs, keeping them open as an expression of receiving.
- Thank God for the gift of his presence; imagine him placing gifts physically in your hands.
- Give thanks for the gift of prayer.
- Receive his friendship and presence.
- Take hold of the gifts of peace, hope, and joy.
- See and feel your sufficiency in Christ for the work of prayer. "You have been given fullness in Christ" (Col. 2:10).

(You may find it helpful to see those gifts as water poured out, which can symbolize life-giving refreshment or the water of baptism that marks us as belonging to Christ.)

Be Still

- Stay in God's presence and enjoy the peace, stillness, and security that are found in him. *(You may "feel" nothing: Faith enables us to trust that we already have these gifts.)*
- Get used to simply being in God's presence—and not having to fill the time with words. *(You may find it helps to say just the four words "Our Father in heaven" slowly and repeatedly.)* Enjoy his presence.

The story is told of an elderly woman, confined to bed, who always had a rosary in her hands, but never "used it": Her hands never moved beyond the first bead. Someone berated her one day for never using her rosary. The elderly woman later shared with a friend: "I never get past those first two words, 'Our Father'; I just hold them in my heart. I never feel like going on."[3]

CHAPTER 2

An Open Door

Prayer as Encounter

The great fact for which all religion stands is the confrontation of the human soul with the transcendent holiness of God.

—John Baillie[1]

Formal moments of prayer are intensified encounters within a continuous process of awareness.

—Jack Dominian[2]

Pray as you can, not as you can't.

—Anonymous

Three themes weave themselves through the pages of Scripture like the threefold cord of Ecclesiastes, which we are told "is not quickly broken" (Eccles. 4:12). They are *story, journey,* and *encounter.*

Story

Scripture is full of story. It is the story of God's existence, of his creation of all that is, and of his revelation to humanity. It is the story of his people and their experience of God. More than this, it is the story of God's visitation by word, by the Word-made-flesh, and the Holy Spirit, with a view to bringing "all things in heaven and on earth together under one head, even Christ" (Eph. 1:10). In short, Scripture can be described as a brief history of eternity.

It is in this story that we find our story, in which our identity is bound up. For each of us has a story. When we say to someone, "Tell me about yourself," they usually tell us their story. The healing power of Scripture is that it gives a context, a setting, and a yardstick by which to measure and interpret our story.

Indeed, baptism is baptism into the story of Jesus. We enter his death and resurrection, are filled with his Spirit, and follow in his footsteps. As we do so we experience Cross-and-Resurrection as a way of life. The pain of broken relationships, and the joy of their restoration. The pain of dashed hopes, and the healing power of new beginnings. The pain of injustice, wounds, and abuse, and the transforming impact of our acceptance "in the Beloved." His story is repeated in the life of the believer.

Journey

The stories that fill the Scriptures, and give meaning and revelation to our stories, are essentially stories of journey—epic journeys.

The first and saddest one is Adam and Eve's journey out of paradise and into darkness. But it is quickly followed by stories filled with hope. The courage of Abraham, who "went, even though he did not know where he was going" (Heb. 11:8); the pain—yet ultimate triumph—of Joseph on his dark journey into Egypt and his "resurrection" to new life in that strange new world. These patriarchal journeys are followed by *the* epic journey of the children of Israel as they made *exodus* (literally "exit") out of the bondage of Egypt to the mount of revelation at Sinai, and on into the promised land, where they become established in their space and become a new people.

The theme of journey continues into exile in Babylon, and back again in a new exodus (the return from exile) under Ezra and Nehemiah, and the prophets' new understanding of holiness and justice.

The New Testament sustains this theme, setting the ministry of Jesus in the context of journey. He calls the disciples to "follow me." Many of Jesus' greatest stories are stories of epic journeys. The stories of the good Samaritan and of the prodigal son are two such journeys which resulted in a different person arriving at the destination from the one who set out.

The heart and climax of the story of Jesus is, of course, the story of a journey—the journey to Jerusalem, and Jesus going "the way of the cross," to Calvary. The risen Lord appearing to the disciples on the road to Emmaus continues into the resurrection era the sense of journey. So in the Acts of the Apostles, it is not surprising to discover that discipleship is called simply "the Way."

We too are on a journey through life. Again, when we want to get to know another person we ask, "Where do you come from?" Our journey gives us our identity. This is why children who have been adopted have a deep longing to find out about their natural parents—and are often eager to meet them. Knowing where I come from tells me who I am.

I love the story of the young mother who, on collecting her six-year-old daughter from school in the car one day, was suddenly posed with the question that parents dread being asked (simply because they do not know how to express the answer): "Mommy, where did I come from?" So, taking a deep breath, as she wove the car in and out of the rush hour traffic across town, she gave as coherent and simple an explanation of the intricacies and delicacies of the human reproductive system as she could. When she reached the end she felt herself settling back in her seat with a sigh of relief and some considerable sense of satisfaction at a job well done. It was not destined to last long, for the voice from the back of the car said, in a dismissive tone of voice, "Yes, Mommy, I know all about that—but I want to know where I came from. Amanda came from Bath, and Jane from Liverpool, where did I come from?"! Knowing where we come from says much about who we are. It gives us our identity.

It is for this reason that testimony plays an important part, not just in Christian witness, but in Christian identity. Telling "how we got here" says much about our understanding of who we are. Indeed, in my recent work I have been looking at what makes churches become life-giving, serving, outward-going communities of faith. One of the books that has helped me most in this work is James Hopewell's book entitled, simply, *Congregation.* His central thesis is that you can only understand a community of believers, and help to bring about change, if you understand the story of their journey—as you listen to their history. In other words, what is true for the individual is true for a community. The story of their journey of faith tells you who and what they are.

Encounter

What makes stories and journeys so interesting and varied are the encounters that take place along the way. They often take place at a crossroad; seemingly chance encounters have a habit of changing the direction in which people are going. That is essentially the nature of a Christian testimony. Testimonies are stories of encounters with God—on the way that led to the Way.

Scripture is full of such encounters.

Jacob wrestles with the angel until he obtains a blessing. It happens on a journey down memory lane—a painful memory lane, as he returns home to put his relationship right with the brother he cheated. A fighter by nature (in the womb and in life), he takes on the angel and is wounded in the thigh. But the wound brings healing. It touches him with his creatureliness, his limits, his need of God's blessing and direction. It is an encounter that changes who he is and the course of his life. It is one of the few encounters in Scripture that takes place in the dark. Yet often, as we shall see in Chapter Six, that is just where we encounter God.

Moses meets God at a burning bush. It is symbolic of Moses' journey to date and the story of the rest of his life. He was a man with a burning sense of justice—hence his action in killing the Egyptian, which resulted in his journey to Midian. It was a high-speed journey, as he literally "ran for his life." Here now he meets a most amazing miracle—something that burns but is not consumed. He sees, and in the encounter that follows, he is touched by a power that includes that burning sense of justice, yet is greater than it, namely, a heart burning with compassion. A compassion that feels and knows and acts.

Mary's encounter with God is another unique event. It really is uniquely unique, if I may put it like that. She is told that she will become mother of the Messiah—without the aid of a human father. No wonder she "pondered these things in her heart." It would take her a lifetime to fathom the meaning of this encounter and subsequent experience. The church today, indeed, is still pondering these things.

For us, too, the story of our journey in faith is punctuated (given form, structure, and meaning) by our encounters with God. In my first book, *In the Crucible,* I begin that story of a church's encounter with God, by telling my own story of some major encounters with God that have shaped who I am and affected all that I have done. Every believer has her or his own unique story to tell.

Prayer as Encounter

What does all this consideration of Scripture being full of stories, journeys, and encounters have to do with prayer? Just this: If discipleship is all about story, journey, and encounter, then this will also be true of prayer. For prayer gives particular focus to, and expression of, our meeting with God.

Notice at this point that the encounters that are recorded in Scripture, although they were of limited duration (only Jacob's, of the ones described above, would have lasted more than a few minutes), they were of lasting impact—like Isaiah's vision in the temple, which constituted his calling to the prophetic ministry. Paul's encounter on the road to Damascus did not last long (falling off a horse takes "no time at all"!), but its impact lasted a lifetime. So with Peter's call to be a fisher of men.

Encounters with God, in other words, shape the nature of discipleship. They are foundational events. They are also model events—they teach us how God reveals himself, and how he can be known on a daily basis. This is why, from both personal experience and study of the Scriptures, I have become convinced that we need to see prayer as encounter with God. It is both one of the fundamental ways in which we meet God, and it is also essential for our reflecting on, and living out our lives in the light of, such major encounters with God as we experience. Moreover, it is how we keep ourselves open to fresh encounters with God—on the Way.

The Structure of Encounters

Having established that life is full of encounters with God, we have already gone some way in answering an objection to seeing encounters as the key to prayer. That objection is that the encounters with God I have referred to are such unique events that there is no consistent pattern that can be seen in them. Certainly at one level that is so. I doubt whether anyone reading this book has seen a burning bush, been knocked off a horse by the revelation of God, or had an annunciation.

However, what I want to show is that there is a clear structure in all of these encounters and that this structure is a fine framework for personal prayer. I want to draw your attention to a threefold pattern that is evident in any type of encounter with God.

It begins with *seeing,* that is, with an awareness of God himself. Transcendent reality breaks through into the lives of ordinary people. The focus is on God, the Other. This is the nature of worship, which involves our being "lost in wonder, love and praise," as the hymn puts it. Awareness of God reorientates us around the fact that God is the center of the world, and of *our* world too. The means will vary enormously—burning bushes, temples filled with God, angels visiting us, and so forth—but the starting point is the same: There is a seeing of the reality and presence of God. This suggests that personal prayer should begin with worship, with looking away, out, and up to God.

Next comes the experience of *knowing* and being known. No one comes out of the experience unchanged. Isaiah is aware of being a man of unclean lips; John on the isle of Patmos "fell at his feet as though dead"; Moses is touched by the justice of God, which does not consume but burns with compassion. There is often a facing up to, owning, and finding transformation from personal sin. Sometimes it is sin that has lain dormant for decades.

Knowing, in the biblical sense, is that intimacy in which we both know and are known. It expresses the deepest level of taking the truth of God into ourselves and being changed by it. So, if the first characteristic of these encounters is that of seeing God, the second is that they address us and bring about change in us. This suggests that worship should be followed by openness to God's Word and Spirit to touch, heal, rebuke, strengthen, affirm, and direct us.

The final stage is that of *going*. Jacob goes to be reconciled to Esau; Moses goes to Pharaoh to say, "Let my people go"; Isaiah responds to the call "who will go for us?" with the declaration "Here am I. Send me!" In the New Testament the same pattern holds. Jesus goes from his baptism to begin his ministry; Peter, after the miraculous catch of fish, goes to be a "fisher of men"; Zacchaeus goes to give back to those whom he has robbed.

Service, and costly discipleship, rather than emotional satisfaction and comfort, is the consistent evidence of true encounter with God. Doubtless some of those events were overwhelmingly emotional experiences, but the goal was not the "feel-good factor" but the "do-good fact." True prayer, equally, will issue in a life of obedience. The Anglican liturgy has it right when, after baptism, it speaks of "fighting under the banner of Christ," and—at the end of the communion service—it sends people out "in the power of your Spirit to live and work to your praise and glory." Such going has two parts. There is the initial part, in personal prayer and public worship, of going through intercession—caring for the world around us; and then there is the physical part—going into the world to participate in God's work.

From a Different Angle

The structure of *seeing, knowing,* and *going* can be described in three words that are rich words in Christian vocabulary: *revelation, conversion,* and *mission.* Indeed, when we see that this is what encounter with God is about we realize that there are few, if any, places in Scripture where at least one of those themes is not evident.

Revelation is the word that Scripture uses to describe how we come to see God. In the me-centered culture in which we live, prayer is easily reduced to technique. The truth is that our seeing God is first and foremost his gift. The word *revelation* also reminds us that those moments of seeing are not so much moments when God turns up, as moments when what is already and always present becomes present to us. Elisha's prayer to God for his servant exactly describes our position. It was not a prayer that God might come, but that the servant might have his eyes opened to see the reality of God's presence: "O LORD, open his eyes so he may see" (2 Kings 6:17).

In our frustrations in prayer (and even biblical characters had them) we can imagine that God is like a camera. He is One whom we can, now and then, imprint a lasting impression on, yet, for the most part, seems shut to the cry of our hearts. The truth is actually the opposite. It is we who are so rarely open. The constant light of God's presence finds limited access to our innermost beings. Like my own camera, we are only open to God for two-hundredths of a second once every other month! As T. S. Eliot put it, "mankind can bear very little reality." However, it is as we look up that we train ourselves to be in the best place to see God, to experience revelation.

Conversion is a word that describes not just a once-in-a-lifetime experience, but a way of life—a life of continual turning to the light of God's presence. With that turning to the light comes change—change in who we are, in how we see life, and in how we resolve to handle it. Paul puts this process of conversion in these terms: "And we, who with unveiled faces all reflect the Lord's glory, are being transformed into his likeness with ever-increasing glory, which comes from the Lord, who is the Spirit" (2 Cor. 3:18). Truly to pray is to be changed in the process. The human instinct is to come to God so as to bring about change in his attitude to us or action for us. True Christian prayer is the prayer "Your kingdom come," and "May it be to me as you have said" (Luke 1:38). As we shall see, the process of turning and being changed is right at the heart of prayer.

Mission is the third word. It points to the fact that there is always a sending out from true encounters with God. It is a sending into his world, his mission, and his will, that we may thereby enter more fully into his presence in the world.

The description in Mark of Jesus' choice of the disciples well expresses this double flow of coming and going that is involved in encounter of God in prayer and life. Mark records: "He appointed twelve—designating them apostles—that they might be with him and that he might send them out" (Mark 3:14). So, for us, being sent out is one of the marks of authentic prayer, to which we will return in due course. More immediately, however, after the prayer exercise that follows, we will explore the first of the elements of encounter, namely, our seeing of God.

Prayer Exercise: Milestones

One of the important purposes of prayer is to help us stop, and be aware of life and what is happening to us, in order that we may make a freely chosen response. This exercise is designed to help us get in touch with our journey of faith so far.

Have pen and paper (better still, a journal) available so that you can write down the things that arise which speak to you. First identify the period "under review." It might be the time of your first encounter with God, but it may well be best to consider the recent past (the past week, month, year), not least because this is something that we can benefit from doing regularly (once every three to six months). For the chosen period, simply review your awareness of what you have experienced and learned over that period, under the three headings of seeing, knowing, and going:

Seeing

In what ways have I been aware of God's presence in my life?

- Is there any experience that stands out?
- Is there something someone said or wrote that has struck a chord in me?
- Is there a Scripture or insight that is memorable?

Make a note of anything, and give thanks for all that is good in your experience.

Knowing

In what ways have I experienced change within myself?

- How have I changed in my attitude to God, myself, or others?
- What are the positive/growth changes?
- Are there any signs of negative or stuck responses in me?

Thank God for his presence in your life, in the joys and the struggles.

Going

In what ways have I been stepping out in faith during this period? Can I identify any sense of going?

- Give thanks to God for that, and reaffirm your commitment to continue.

Are there ways in which I have sensed God's call to go, but not yet gone?

- Bring that before God, affirming your confidence in his ability to help.

Are there ways that you sense God sending you out in the light of this time?

- to say something to someone
- to take some deliberate action

Note it and be specific about when, where, and how action can be taken.

Note: This is not to be an inquisition in which you criticize yourself for how you have failed, but rather a trusting review before the One who is for you. The purpose is to listen more fully to the One who is Love.

Part 2

SEEING

Chapter 3

Ways into Seeing

> He counted addiction to prayer not so much the aid of his episcopate as the delight of his soul.
>
> —said of a cardinal in the Vatican at the time of the Reformation

Worship is a form of orienteering, for we travel through life like a blind person finding his or her way along a street. Such a person will be rehearsing how many paces before the curb, where the next lamp post is, and where to turn right. Worship has such a role in the life of the believer. It reminds us where we are. Worship puts us in touch with the things that help and guide us, alerts us to what is harmful, and points us to the Center of the universe—and of our lives. It is orienteering in a universe where physical sight is dangerous, because we easily conclude that what you see is what you get. In fact, as Elisha's servant found out, there is a holy art to true seeing (2 Kings 6), which is itself a gift of God. We can confidently ask for the gift of such seeing. As Paul puts it:

> So we fix our eyes not on what is seen, but on what is unseen. For what is seen is temporary, but what is unseen is eternal.
>
> —2 Corinthians 4:18

What we have established so far is that the first stage in a true meeting with God begins with God himself, and with our *seeing* him. To see God is to recognize him for who he is, the Sovereign Lord, "high and exalted" (Isa. 6:1), as Isaiah expresses it. Seeing God as the center of the universe, and therefore as the center of my world of relationships and responsibilities, is to be converted: turned around to see the One from whom all life comes. It is also liberation from self-centeredness. This is why, in every age, the first requirement for the creature is to acknowledge the Creator. This is so, not because *he* needs our worship, but because *we* do.

How does this work out in the prayer life of the Christian today? Here we turn to the practice of worship, or *seeing* as I have called it, in the pattern of our prayer encounter with God. In the next chapter we will explore one particular way in which we can "enter his courts with praise." It is based on Revelation 4 and 5 and is called "beholding the throne." Here, however, I want to explore other ways in which we can train ourselves to focus first on God, before proceeding further in prayer.

The Celebration of Stillness

We live in a frantic world, where we are in danger of losing touch with the sheer gift of life. We risk the possibility of becoming "human doings" rather than "human beings." So we need to relearn what it is to live in the moment, to receive life as a gift to be enjoyed rather than as a problem to be solved, and to enjoy who we are and what we have received. In other words, we need to learn how to celebrate Sabbath. Not only did God rest on the seventh day, but throughout creation we are told that "he saw that it was good" (Gen. 1:10, 12, 18, 21, 25, concluding with v. 31, "God saw all that he had made, and it was very good"). He took time to meditate on all his works, to enjoy the process as much as the product.

One way for us to "step out of ourselves" is to still our hearts, look up to God, and slowly and quietly give thanks for all that is. Yes, it is all right to begin with ourselves. Thank God for our breathing, for such health and mental faculties as we have. But we go beyond that, making connection with all that is. This is what the Old Testament concept of shalom—peace—is all about. This can include the warmth and furnishing of the room, our "loved ones," and human society. We can thank God for the gift of the government. That might seem like a difficult task, but a moment's reflection on the recent history of Lebanon and the former state of Yugoslavia reminds us all too vividly of the hell of no government.

Beyond that, we can step out and make connection with creation, whether as expressed in pictures on our walls, or pictures in our prayer journal (yes, put in the "views" that speak to you), or simply in our imagination. It may not just be a view as such (e.g., Mount Everest), but rather a location that we associate with an experience of connectedness with all that is—a moment of shalom.

Little, if any, of this needs to be with spoken words. We can practice looking, remembering, and imagining, with praise and gratitude to the Creator and Giver of the gifts we are enjoying.

In this way we are stilling our hearts, stopping the rush of modern society that disorientates us, and coming in touch with the child within. And we need a little child to lead us, for it is the child who knows how to play, how to enjoy the present moment, and how to be in touch with the wonder of it all. If we do use words, it could be by repeating, from the liturgy "Lift up your hearts, we lift them to the Lord" as the only words we use while making this journey of adoration to the Author of life. In so doing we discover him restoring in us the capacity to wonder, to enjoy, and to be still. Above all, this journey out from self to the Center needs to take us through connection with all created reality, into the presence of the Creator and Giver of All.

Devotional Psalms

Another, and more familiar, way of entering into God's presence is to make use of the devotional psalms. The more I have studied the psalms and discussed their use with people, the more I have become convinced that the list of such psalms is not as fixed as one might think. Some people find one psalm devotional and others not. By "devotional" I mean a psalm that takes us into God—turns our attention to him and assists our *seeing* him. We will see, in Chapter Seven ("Praying Back the Scriptures"), more about how best to pray the Scriptures—rather than just read them. However, for those not familiar with such a list here are the first dozen I use: Psalms 8, 16, 19, 23, 24, 25, 27, 29, 33, 34, 40, 42. It would be best for you, however, to develop your own list.

The Psalms have always played a large part in the spiritual disciplines and prayer life of the church. It is clear from Jesus' prayer life that the Psalms were both his Prayer Book and his Hymn Book. The monastic movement has made the use of the Psalms a major feature of its daily worship. Indeed, some parts of the Orthodox Church used to require of anyone seeking ordination, that they be able to recite from memory all 150 psalms! Certainly we can benefit greatly if we learn some psalms by heart, and pray them with our heart. It is then quite possible to use the psalm while driving, or having a bath, or whatever, because we have it written on our heart. I use Psalm 45 like this. Not that I claim to know it word for word, but—as we shall see below—I know the structure and the content sufficiently that it spurs on worship in my own words.

The Liturgy of the Heart

Here I want to pause to spell out a second prayer principle that can aid us greatly in this work: the liturgy of the heart. It may sound strange to some people's ears that liturgy and the heart have any connection—especially in the context of personal prayer. But they do, or rather they can, in the following way.

There is an ancient liturgical principle on which, for example, the Anglican Church has built not just its worship but its doctrine too. The principle, in its Latin form, is *lex orandi, lex credendi,* which means *"the word spoken is the word believed."* The principle is that what we say regularly and build into our unconscious and subconscious has a powerful and formative effect on us. It shapes our thinking, behavior, and belief. It is for this reason that the Anglican Church does not have a doctrinal basis, for it sees that its doctrine is enshrined in its liturgy.

> **Prayer Principle 2**
>
> **Write the Truth in Our Hearts**
>
> Learning prayers by heart plants truths as seeds within that can help us to enjoy their fruit at any time.

Many people today—particularly those influenced by charismatic renewal—falsely imagine that the only form of prayer is spontaneous prayer. That is an important element of prayer, but so is the prayer of the heart that arises out of what we have consciously sown in it. If we will but write things that really matter in our hearts, we will find them becoming a well of living water, especially when we are in desert places.

Sight: Using an Icon

Here is one of those spiritual exercises I referred to in the introduction. Sadly, for many of us in the West, and especially those nurtured in the evangelical and renewal traditions of the church, we have become deeply captive to the culture in ways we often miss. In particular, we have become trapped within a narrowly rational way of understanding reality, and into a consequent restriction of communication to words alone. Yes, the Word of God is foundational to the gospel and to Christian living. Yes, God and creation can be understood—to some degree—by rational thought. But we have lost sight of the greater truth of the Word-made-flesh. Jesus, after all, is the living icon (image/likeness) of the Father (Heb. 1:3).

Prayer of the Heart

Seeing God

Holy God, holy and mighty,
Holy and immortal,
Have mercy on us.

—The trisagion (thrice-holy) chant
of the Orthodox Church
which has been sung for
well over one thousand years

We tend to take icons too literally. We only see them as *pictures.* We need to know that this is not how the Orthodox Church handles them. In that tradition people are told: "When you pray, stand before an icon, *close your eyes,* and pray to the Father in heaven." That should alert us to the fact that something other than the worship of the icon is going on.

We are instructed to close our eyes because an icon is seen not as a picture on the wall, but as a *window* into heaven. We are to "see through" (as we say) the icon—seeing through to the truth portrayed in it. Jesus was doing this all the time in his parables. He was seeing through the fragile existence of the sparrow to the faithfulness of the One who cares for it; he was seeing through the work of the sower, to the greater work of the Sower of all creation and creativity.

Indeed, even *window* is not sufficient to describe the role of icons, for they are intended to be a *door* that leads us into the presence of God. They fulfill the role of the open door in heaven through which John "saw" the glory of heaven's praises—as we shall see in the next chapter. So too, an icon can lead us into the presence of God.

The Oaks of Mamre

Consider, for example, one of the best known icons in the West at present—Rublev's icon called "The hospitality of Abraham." It represents the story of the three visitors whom Abraham and Sarah had when they "entertained angels unawares" (Genesis 18). Those visitors came to tell them that they would have a son within the year—at which news Sarah laughed.

Orthodox spirituality sees in those visitors a picture of the Trinity. Rublev represents them sitting before a table with a chalice on it (remember, Abraham went and killed an animal for the meal). On the right-hand side is a figure clothed in green and blue robes. Those robes represent the green of earth and the blue of heaven. It is the figure of the Holy Spirit. He is both the One who comes from heaven (blue), as the communicator of divinity to humanity, and yet also the One at home on earth (green), for he was the agent of creation when the world was made and when the Son was conceived (Gen. 1:2; Luke 1:35). He is the One who introduces us to the Godhead.

In this icon, the figure representing the Holy Spirit has his head bowed toward the person in the center, robed partly in blue and partly in the royal robes of empire. This is the figure of Jesus, the One who, in a unique way came from heaven, but who now has returned to glory as the all-conquering king who overcame through death, defeating evil by the power of unselfish, sacrificial, and forgiving love. His head is also bowed, as he looks to the figure on the left of the picture.

This third figure is robed in translucent robes that speak of an inner glory that shines forever. Here the Father is seated in majesty, yet also as the One who visits this earth. Remember, "*God* was reconciling the world to himself in Christ" (2 Cor. 5:19, my italics).

These figures are seated in a circle, but it is not a completed or closed circle. It is a *C,* not an *O.* The whole picture invites us in—to complete the circle, to be part of the life of mutual love, affirmation, and creativity that characterizes the interaction within the Trinity. What an immense and incredible privilege. This is the source of vitality for all living. No wonder we can simply stand before such a presence and, without a word, enter in through the door of adoration.

Delight

A further way into the presence of God, which enables us to take delight in the Lord (Ps. 37:4; a phrase worth studying throughout the psalm as an aid to worship itself), is by means of the image of marriage as it applies to the church's relationship with God. It is a picture used widely in Scripture.

Psalm 45 is a wedding psalm that I also call an "encounter psalm" for it expresses the three phases of encounter. The first part of the psalm (45:1–9) sings the praises of the king who is about to be married: This is the *seeing* phase. The next part of the psalm (45:10–15) is addressed to the bride, who through marriage is about to have her whole identity changed and bound up with that of the king: This is the *knowing and being known* phase of encounter with God. The last part (45:16–17) speaks of the fruit of this union, the children who will be born to the royal couple: This is the *going* phase of encounter. It is a wonderful psalm for reorientating ourselves around the reality of God and his love for us.

The Song of Songs is a whole book devoted to the love relationship of marriage. It found a place in Scripture partly because the Jewish people were at home in creation and the natural world—they did not suffer from the dualism evident in the Greek culture that has so influenced our present way of seeing life. That Greek notion made such a distinction between the physical and spiritual that it created a conflict between them. To the Hebrew mind reality can be seen as having layers of meaning bound up in the one event, the physical in the spiritual and the spiritual in the physical. The Hebrew mind was well able to see God and his goodness and generosity mirrored in human loving. However, there was another reason for the book's presence in the Old Testament Scriptures. It was included because it was seen as describing the relationship between Israel and God.

The marriage theme is continued throughout the New Testament. Jesus speaks of himself as the Bridegroom whom the disciples will not always have with them (Mark 2:19). Paul, in writing about the marriage relationship, points beyond it in his great passage in Ephesians, when he concludes with the words: "This is a profound mystery—but I am talking about Christ and the church" (Eph. 5:32). He also uses the marriage relationship in a striking way in Romans (7:1–4). Finally, Scripture ends with the vision of the marriage supper of the Lamb, and "the new Jerusalem, coming down out of heaven from God, prepared as a bride beautifully dressed for her husband" (Rev. 21:2).

On several occasions in my prayer pilgrimage I have used Watchman Nee's little commentary, *The Song of Songs* (Christian Literature Crusade, London, '65), to take me through that book, a little at a time. It took about three months the last time I did it; after all, why rush a good meal? To take delight in the Lord is to enjoy both him and his love for us. Prayer is an experience, quite intense at times—although often, in my experience, not for long—in which we encounter Love in its richest form.

We need to slow down, however, if we are to touch such moments; for they are part of God's good plan for us. Sadly we are often in so much of a hurry that we rush into God's presence, deliver our message (about our need, or our preferred solution to some issue), and depart, without ever having said "hello" or enjoyed the One who loves us.

Silence

There is a certain progression in the stages of seeing God which are built into the logic of the steps we have been through, from celebration through psalms, and sight, to delight and silence. The important point is to be aware of these elements, for then we shall be able to recognize the voice of the One who loves us when we realize he is calling us on into delight or silence.

I have little to say about silence. After all, words seem hardly appropriate, but I have recently seen that it is not so much a straight line, from celebration to silence, as a circle. For silence encapsulates the capacity to be still and to enjoy the present moment—as the Moment of the Presence. So we need to do some "stillness" exercises.

I have found some of the following helpful. For a number of months, I carried around this quotation from Dr. Clyde Kilby, which helped me to still the inner turmoil and the instinctive rushing on to the "next business":

> Once every day I shall simply stare at a tree, a flower, a cloud, or a person. I shall not then be concerned at all to ask *what* they are but simply be glad *that* they are.[1]

Another exercise is to read the poem that follows, simply as a way of slowing down. It says, at one level, nothing about God or worship, or adoration. Yet God reveals himself in the whole of his creation—as does any artist—and we do indeed meet him there. Yet I do not read the poem *in order to meet God*—that turns it into technique and discipline. I read it rather to slow myself down, to enter into delight, into the present moment, and into awareness of the wonder of creation. For that is a place where God so often is discovered. Such an exercise in stillness leads me into celebration and so back into the other ways of seeing. May that be your experience too. Track the steps and paths that God takes you on as you take delight in the Lord and learn to "be still, and know that I am God" (Ps. 46:10):

> What is this life if full of care,
> We have no time to stand and stare?
>
> No time to stand beneath the boughs
> and stare as long as sheep and cows.

No time to see, when woods we pass,
where squirrels hide their nuts in grass:

No time to see in broad daylight,
streams full of stars, like skies at night:

No time to turn at Beauty's glance,
And watch her feet, how they can dance:

No time to wait till her mouth can
Enrich that smile her eyes began?

A poor life this, if full of care,
We have no time to stand and stare.

—William Henry Davies, *Leisure*

Prayer Exercise: Calling on the Name of the Lord

This is a way of developing what I call a liturgy of the heart. Words and forms of prayer are so written on our hearts that they spring up like wells of living water from within us. Another name for this exercise is the *grammar of praise,* for it focuses on:

- *nouns,* the names we give God
- *adjectives,* which describe the way we see God's character
- *verbs,* which tell how we see God at work

The exercise concludes with our response of adoration, in words, or silent enjoyment and seeing of God.

> *Sit down, relax your body, let go of distracting thoughts and tasks, and receive and welcome God's presence—by faith, whatever the feelings are.*

His Name Is Wonderful

Now call on the name of the Lord by repeating the following titles of God: Rock, Light, Shepherd, Friend, Creator.

Repeat them slowly, savoring them, picturing the title used and then moving to the next one. Once you have these five names you can develop two further exercises.

(a) Add your response: after "Shepherd," for example, you may want to say "thank you that you know me by name" and "thank you that you care." Keep your response short; do not strive in any way. If words dry up, move back into the rhythm of the names.

(b) Add your own list of names (or substitute them for the ones suggested).

The Holy One

Next (at the same "sitting," or at another time, maybe after a month of doing the first part), do the same exercise, this time focusing on God's character. Here is the list to get you started:

holy, joyful, faithful, creative, mighty.

Again, take the words slowly.

- Take them into yourself, memorizing them and chewing them over.
- Add your own further adjectives and responses as before.

The God Who Acts

The final part is as above, but uses verbs to describe what God does. Here is the list to get you started:

The One who sets free, shakes, calls, speaks, loves.

- Think of words that tell us who he is, what his character is, and how he reveals himself to us.

Chapter 4

Beholding the Throne

> The way to overcome gravity—and so much triviality—is to arise in the Presence each morning.
>
> —David Adam[1]

> Forfeit your sense of awe, let your conceit diminish your ability to revere, and the universe becomes a marketplace for you.
>
> —Rabbi Heschel[2]

While worship is essential to life, holiness, and health in every age, there are two particular reasons why this is especially true today.

Over the course of the past few hundred years there has been a strange twist in the development of human consciousness and the human perception of reality—at least in Western culture. It is this. When people thought that the earth was the center of the universe, with the sun, moon, and stars all orbiting around Planet Earth, they had no difficulty in grasping the fact that God is the true center of all created order, and that—for sheer survival—we are to give God his rightful worship and the obedience of our lives to his revealed will.

Yet, since scientists discovered that the earth is just one of several planets circling one not particularly special star, somewhat to the edge of a galaxy which is part of a family of millions of galaxies, we have—at a deep psychological level—functioned as though *we* are the center of the world. Or rather, because of our individualism, we instinctively act as though *I* am the center of reality. This self-centered view of reality is one of the primary characteristics of our culture.

It is therefore vital that we break out of this false notion. We need today to be converted from the surrounding culture's view of reality, to the truth that God is the center of all that is. In an address in 1993 to the Congress of European Bishops, Cardinal Basil Hume said:

> In a world that is seen by many to have no ultimate purpose or value, the Self is seen as providing the only realm in which our experience can have meaning. No authority external to the individual is acknowledged.

Indeed, the Christian community needs to be aware of how far this self-centered view of reality has permeated our thinking. Tom Smail, in his book *The Forgotten Father,* expresses well how this worldview has affected the renewal movement:

> The crucial question that the whole renewal faces is whether renewed people will be led only as far as their own felt needs take them, or whether they will go on in obedience to the Father who wants to make them a sign to the world of his transforming and revolutionary power in Christ.
>
> —Tom Smail[3]

Spiritual Orientation

Another reason worship is needed as a healing gift in our culture is that the trends toward secularization and materialism have eaten away at the sense of awe, wonder, and transcendence that are all around us in the universe, and for which the human spirit hungers.

An African bishop once said, "You Westerners are so busy counting your pennies, you have lost the art of counting your blessings!" We have lost touch with the spiritual dimension of all reality. But things are changing—although not necessarily for the better. There is now a growing spiritual awareness, hunger, and interest in our society. However, because it is happening in the context of a self-focused, self-aware, and self-centered culture, there is an inevitable tendency to look for that spiritual dimension within. This is the basis of New Age spirituality.

Typical of this approach was the comment of the leader of a New Age community, who said on TV that, as she listened to the voices within her, she realized not just that this was God, but that, as she put it, "as Jesus said, 'the Father and I are one,' so I now realize that I am my own divinity. I do not need to look outside for the Divine." That horrific misreading of Scripture, and of one's own nature, is best addressed by a strong focus on the Otherness and transcendent glory of God. This is where prayer must begin.

Yes, God does dwell with us, and in us. Yet he is also, and essentially, beyond us and other than us. In technical terms, his immanence is a consequence of his prior transcendence. In other words, God exists before, beyond, and apart from his creation, before he becomes present to it and to us humans in it. His presence flows out of his Otherness. Once we let go of the fact that he is our Father in *heaven,* we become disconnected from him and turn our search toward "the divine within." Indeed, I see that this could become the Achilles heel of the charismatic movement with its love of an informality that domesticates God.

We are in urgent need of seeing God in his transcendent glory. This is why the discipline of looking away from self and seeing God is vital to prayer, and to our sheer survival as worshiping creatures.

One Particular Way

The practice of beholding the throne is based on Revelation 4 and 5, which reveal the worship of God in eternity. It takes us into the realm of the unseen, which is the true and unchanging reality. The focus of that world is the glory of the Father, the wonder of the Lamb slain from the foundation of the world, and the sevenfold active presence of the Holy Spirit.

In taking this outer-directed step of focus on God, it is important to remember that Jesus not only taught us to begin our prayers by saying, "Our Father in heaven," but also began his own prayers in the same way. For example at the conclusion of the mission of the disciples, Jesus prays: "I praise you, Father, Lord of heaven and earth" (Matt. 11:25). In his prayer as recorded in John 17, we are told: "After Jesus said this, he looked toward heaven and prayed: 'Father . . .'" (John 17:1). Revelation 4 and 5 simply gives us a permanent record of the heavenly vision that was, for a moment, opened up to Isaiah (Isaiah 6). It is now written down for our instruction.

As we behold the throne we are doing what the apostle Paul told us to do:

> set your hearts on things above, where Christ is seated at the right hand of God.
>
> —Colossians 3:1

The writer of the epistle to the Hebrews encourages us in similar words when he writes:

> fix your thoughts on Jesus, the apostle and high priest whom we confess.
>
> —Hebrews 3:1

> Let us fix our eyes on Jesus, the author and perfecter of our faith.
>
> —Hebrews 12:2

To do so is to be liberated from self-concern and self-centeredness, and to enter more fully into likeness to Christ. This is the law of unconscious assimilation. We become like those whom we spend most meaningful and frequent time with.

Like exiles, we long for our homeland ("our citizenship is in heaven," Phil. 3:20). As we behold the throne we live in the "presence of the future." We are preparing, as the exiles of eternity (1 Peter 1:1–2), for the everlasting worship of God in heaven.

Brief Overview

It is helpful to have some understanding of the place of these two chapters in the book of Revelation, and of the way in which they balance each other.

John, suffering persecution and imprisonment for the faith along with many others, is on the isle of Patmos. There he has a vision of Christ in glory. This encounter with the risen Lord causes him to fall down as if dead. However, he is raised up to be told that he is about to see "what is to come," with a view to his sharing that with the embattled churches of the region. He then receives an individual letter for each of those seven churches—letters that are incisive, affirming, and specific to each location.

After this personal encounter, and these words to the local churches, the scene moves to the glory of heaven. That is the focus of chapters 4 and 5, to which we will return shortly. After those chapters comes a series of bewildering (to the modern reader) and graphic visions of the spiritual conflict of the end times, culminating in the fall of Babylon (Rome, symbol of the principalities and powers), the marriage supper of the Lamb, the coming of the new Jerusalem and the invitation of the Spirit and Bride to come into the kingdom prepared for those who are called.

Chapters 4 and 5 are therefore the hinge chapters. Chapter 4 begins with an open door, through which John steps and sees the glory of all that is. He sees the creative, yet unchanging, reality of heaven.

The key to chapter 4 is that everything is seen in relation to the throne. In meditating on it, it has the power to integrate our living and give us connectedness with all that is.

The mood changes in chapter 5. There is a great sense of *being* in chapter 4. Chapter 5 is about *doing,* about the work of creation and the re-creation of everything through the death and resurrection of Christ (the Lamb). The key is the opening of the scroll, which is the symbol of the unfolding of God's purposes in his world. The grief that John experiences is because there seems to be no one who can open those scrolls (that is, fulfill God's plan for his world). Grief turns to joy with the arrival of the Lion of the tribe of Judah.

Chapter 4 then, before the throne, celebrates the being of God as Center of all that is. Chapter 5 explains the unfolding of his redeeming work in history. This balance of being and doing defines the nature of the whole cosmos—stillness of being, and purposefulness in creativity—and our natures too. As we meditate on these Scriptures we are put in touch with these sources of healing life by relationship to the One from whom they come.

Entering in with the Imagination

What follows is designed to help us enter, in imagination and spirit, into the center of reality and in the process to be reorientated around unseen reality, through meditation on Revelation 4 and 5.

Here we need some muscle-stretching prayer exercise. The muscles I refer to are our imaginations. For the fact is that modern life leaves little or nothing to the imagination; it does it all for us. This is partly because our culture has been very rational (although this is now changing). So, typically today, when we read, we read "literally." We are at home with the handbook for the video or the freezer. It tells us the mechanics of how the thing works. It requires no imagination to read. Likewise our entertainment leaves little to the imagination—not least in the literal portrayal of sex and violence. As a society, our imagination has been starved, and our ability to imagine has atrophied. This is where the Holy Spirit comes to our aid in prayer. It is the Spirit who enables us to feel, and sense, and imagine a situation. It is the Spirit who helps when we find our imagination weak (Rom. 8:26, 27).

Practical Matters

Here again, the principle of "counting the steps," being the stage before dancing, is an important one to bear in mind. In other words, do not be surprised if you find this exercise "awkward," "self-conscious," "artificial," or "not me." That is an inevitable part of the learning phase.

The first stage is to use the words given, and then—as you make them your own—use a prayer journal to record your own thoughts and ways of meditating. You may find it helpful to write out simply the text of Scripture given below on a page or two of your journal, and then add your own commentary or "aid to meditation" yourself. What follows is intended to get your imagination started. As we have already seen, it is important to write the text of Scripture on our hearts. I am now able to sit on a bus or train, and enter into this meditation, simply because I have done it often enough to have the Scriptures on instant recall.

You may also find it helpful to take one section at a time and meditate on it over several prayer times before moving on to the next. When I began doing it I did the first section for a few weeks, and then added the second, and then the third. To make it manageable I then dropped the first and added the fourth. Eventually I got to the last section, by which time I was still doing only three at a time. As you work on this material over a sustained period (a number of weeks) you will find it becoming increasingly your own. You will then need the notes less and less, and will be able to find your own way more and more.

John Talbot, founder of the Brothers and Sisters of Charity, has the following wise and encouraging words to say about this repeated engaging with, and memory of, Scripture:

> One of the ways to control the mind is by good Christian meditation. This means taking the time intentionally to fill our minds and thoughts with the ways of Jesus Christ. This is done by meditating on the Scriptures. . . . When we do this as an intentional discipline, we discover that our thoughts will soon begin going to Jesus on their own in their wanderings. Once we train the mind to take this journey through intentional discipline, it will begin doing it on its own by way of habit.
>
> —John Talbot[4]

Prayer Principle 3

Sowing and Reaping Take Time

In our mechanical world we expect the light to come on as soon as we flick the switch.

Prayer functions in the realm of relationships and growing things.

You reap what you sow—but not the same day!

Growing things take time to develop.

Sowing requires faith.

However, remember that internalizing these things does take time. How often did you repeat your multiplication tables before they became part of you? Beholding the throne is a more difficult, and more vital, task, but it happens in the same way.

Repeat each verse of Scripture several times, read the meditation slowly seeking to see and enter into this vision, repeating the Scripture as frequently as you feel comfortable with. End by saying the Scripture by heart. Do not be concerned to meditate and memorize; become comfortable with the memorizing first, and then the meditation on the Scripture will grow.

Prayer Exercise: Beholding the Throne

There before me was a door standing open. . . . "Come up here, and I will show you what must take place after this" (Rev. 4:1).

- See the open door as large and looking out onto a vast (outdoor) scene.

We are not entering in, so much as coming out in the open, to enjoy God and all that is.

- Hear the open invitation: the angel's summons to come.

It is personal, caring, yet with great (divine) authority. Sense the honor of the invitation; you have personally been called before God.

- Be aware that this is a journey in time, to gain a foretaste of where the world is going.

Know that you have this foretaste of the destination to help you recognize the Way there.

This is a glimpse of glory, of what is lasting in life, and of where you are heading.

At once I was in the Spirit (Rev. 4:2a).

- Relax; prayer is the gift of God.
- See yourself as in a sailing boat carried by the wind of the Spirit into the Father's presence.

"I am a feather in the breath of God," said St. Hildegarde of Bingen.

- See yourself carried by the Spirit, into the glory of what is to come.

Remember the icon of the Trinity and that the Spirit is drawing you into the unending flow of love, and unity, and creativity in the Godhead.

There before me was a throne in heaven with someone sitting on it (Rev. 4:2b).

- Rejoice. All that is, is no accident; there is a Hand on the helm of the universe.

There is a throne, and One who is in control. It is none other than the "God and Father of our Lord Jesus Christ." Everything in this passage is related to the throne ("surrounding," "from," "before," etc.).

Let the tide of this reality flood out into your life and world. Everything that is finds its identity in relation to God.

- Sense the awe and wonder of this divine Center of all that is.

Feel the vastness of the universe, finding its point of origin, direction, and meaning from the Person who is seated on the throne.

The One who sat there had the appearance of jasper and carnelian. A rainbow, resembling an emerald, encircled the throne (Rev. 4:3).

- Color is now added to our vision of God in glory.
    - See the rich colors building to the center of the universe.

    Let the richness of color shake you free of any dull vision of God.

    - He is the source of life and light and glory and joy and wonder.

    Creation reflects something of the brilliance of his being.

    - Do not try to "work out" how a rainbow can be green (emerald), but rejoice in the brilliance and beauty of all creation.

    See the beauty of any part of creation that has touched you, coming before God to worship him.

Surrounding the throne were twenty-four . . . elders. They were dressed in white and had crowns of gold on their heads (Rev. 4:4).

- How wonderful that humanity is included, not excluded, by God's presence.
    - What cost he bore to count us in on his eternal purposes.

    The elders are the patriarchs of the Old Covenant, and the apostles of the New. They are our patriarchs and apostles: we rejoice for them, and in them. Imagine the look in their eyes, their love for God, their rejoicing in the end of the story of which they were such a vital part.

- Know that God counts all believers in on that same story.

He clothes us with righteousness so that we can enter. The robes he has put on us are not for outward show, but robes that penetrate the heart.

From the throne came flashes of lightning, rumblings and peals of thunder (Rev. 4:5).

- Creation is gathered up into God's presence together with:
    - the vastness of space
    - the depths of the ocean
    - the molten fire a thousand miles thick that begins twenty miles below our feet
    - the delicacy of the desert flower and the beauty of the sea horse
- The trees of the field and the rivers clap their hands.
    - The roaring lion gives praise to God, as do the planets singing on their way.
    - Even the stones cry out to the source of all being. Know that this overwhelming power is always and only used in love.
    - As fallen humanity we are trapped and diminished by the love of power.
    - In divine glory we are touched and made whole by the power of love.
- See this holy and loving power as able to gather up the most broken parts of creation and
    - bring *it to wholeness in Christ.*
- All creation is gathered up in the vision of God on the throne.
    - In Christ, we are all part of this amazing end times scene.
    - Now we see it with our imagination; one day we will literally enter in.

Before the throne, seven lamps were blazing. These are the seven spirits of God (Rev. 4:5).

- See the Spirit as so all-enveloping and active that he can only be described by the perfect number—seven.

  He is fire: the fire that does not consume, the fire of the burning bush and the fire of the burning fiery furnace that did not consume, the fire within Jesus on the Mount of Transfiguration, and the fire that fell at Pentecost. He is light, shining love and truth into our lives and wisdom on the path before us.

- There is no darkness of human distress, evil, destructiveness, and injustice he cannot penetrate with light. See that light entering the dark places you are aware of in the world.

In the center, around the throne, were four living creatures, and they were covered with eyes (Rev. 4:6).

- As the cherubim on the ark of the covenant witnessed to the presence of the Creator of all, so now these creatures witness to God's redeeming purposes for all creation,

to bring all things in heaven and on earth together under one head, even Christ (Eph. 1:10).

- Rejoice in this good news for a suffering world.

The whole creation has been groaning as in the pains of childbirth (Rom. 8:22).

- Let the hope of Christ's return lighten your heart with the good that is to come.

The creation waits in eager expectation for the children of God to be revealed (Rom. 8:19).

"Do not weep! See, the Lion of the tribe of Judah, the Root of David, has triumphed" (Rev. 5:5).

- Feel the distress of John, that "no one was found who was worthy to open the scroll."
- Then rejoice with him as he hears afresh this proclamation of the gospel.

- Marvel that the Lion and the Lamb lie down together in the person of Christ (Rev. 5:5–6).
- Enter into the continual celebration in heaven that the victory has been won.

We are on the winning side, and the best is yet to be. By our baptism we have participated in Christ's victory and have been taken up into heaven to rejoice and be with him.

The four living creatures said, "Amen," and the elders fell down and worshiped (Rev. 5:14).

■ Lift up your heart in praise to God for who he is and what he has done.

- Join in the celebration of all creation.

Remember that "Amen" is a triumphant "yes" to all God's purposes, nature, and work.

* * * * *

Scattered in the text of these two chapters are the five songs of Revelation 4 and 5—they are affirmation of God's glory:

- The first two speak of God as the Creator of all (Rev. 4:8 and 4:11).
- The second two speak of Jesus as Redeemer (Rev. 5:9–10 and 5:12).
- The last one speaks of Father and Son in all their glory as Creator and Redeemer (Rev. 5:13).

Each of these songs is rightly the basis for meditative entering into the glory of God in their own right and can form the basis of a complete exercise of seeing God. Take time to savor them and be at home in their truths, which pull us out of ourselves into holy self-forgetfulness.

Part 3

KNOWING

CHAPTER 5

Called by Love

Finding Ourselves through Encounter with God

There can be no love of others, much less love of God unless there is a self to do the loving.

—Roberta Bondi[1]

We can desire to become the Beloved only when we know that we already are the Beloved.

—Henri Nouwen[2]

Prayer is an affair of the heart, the primary means of both discovering our identity and yet not being bound by it. Personal health and growth involves both aspects of the paradox of being sure of who I am and becoming different. That paradox was well expressed in a prayer meeting I attended a number of years ago. Someone prayed, "Lord, we thank you for accepting us just as we are." It was a valid and important truth to express to God in prayer. However, it was followed immediately with the heartfelt response of another person who prayed: "And thank you, Lord, for not leaving us where we are."

Self-acceptance and openness to change are vital ingredients of prayer. We will explore both in this chapter, for prayer, like any intimate relationship, has built into it the dynamic of the heart's hunger, expressed in the cry, "Tell me who I am."

Discovering Identity in Prayer

Modern people are profoundly shaped by a man whose name they may never have heard of—Descartes. René Descartes was a seventeenth-century philosopher who propounded the dictum, "I think, therefore I am." It has had an amazing impact on how we in the Western world see and understand ourselves. In propounding that dictum, Descartes was saying that we find our identity within. We are the starting point of our own identity.

Scripture, and modern psychology, disagree. Both argue that we are beings-in-relationship, who discover our identity through relationship. The foundational relationship is with our primary caregivers—normally our parents. It is they who, in a multitude of ways, both give us permission to be ourselves and help us to discover who we are. They call us into being.

Or they fail to do that. Families where such healthy identity is not discovered are called "dysfunctional families"; they simply do not do the basic job they are designed for and can have a crippling effect on a person's being and well-being. This is where the good news of God's love comes in. His love calls us into being. It is without variation, it is not meeting its own needs, and it gives us permission and encouragement to discover and be who we are.

If we have traveled any distance in seeing God, as explored in Part 2, then it will have been having its effect on our self-understanding. Because we are beings-in-relationship we tend to be "different" with each person to whom we relate. This can be destructive, if we are trying to control everyone we meet, because we end up having "no fixed abode" within.

It can also be a sign of health and a gift to our health. If everyone we meet draws out of us some aspect of our nature, then life will enrich us at every turn—yes, even if what another person draws out of us is our anger and frustration! What makes the difference? It is that there is a secure "self to do the loving," as Roberta Bondi puts it.

Our parents do stand as God-substitutes, or divine signposts at least, in our early years, for they lay the foundations on which we build our own self-understanding and self-acceptance. However, it is in relationship to God alone that we can truly find our identity, which is why our seeing of God can have such profound healing effects on us. It lifts us out of introspection to focus on the Other who is truly Center of all that is. In the very act of doing so, we find ourselves. This is well expressed in a book on worship by three authors who say:

> Worship is enjoying God. In worship our attention is directed away from ourselves, to God and to our neighbor. We do not "enjoy ourselves" in worship, indeed the very opposite; at the start we look at ourselves honestly and confess our sins, then as forgiven sinners we can cease to be absorbed by self and open out to God and his glory, and our neighbor and his needs.

Sin, according to a phrase much used by Augustine and Luther, means being *incurvatus in se,* turning in on self. C.S. Lewis found an amazing release from this obsession with self when he was given the capacity of enjoying God and consequently his neighbor.

—Forrester/McDonald/Tellini[3]

Lost or Found?

The parable of the prodigal son is the story of someone making a journey of discovery about his true identity and "home." It has a particular relevance to modern Western culture.

The journey begins through seeking independence from all relationships—the cry for freedom. But although the gift of freedom is given by the Father, the discovery of the true self is not found. The prodigal is adrift on a chartless sea of experiences in relationships that give no identity or meaning. So too for us. We are in an uncharted sea of individuality in which no authority or relationship beyond the self can have a shaping significance. It is not surprising that loneliness is a major sickness of our culture. Included in this search is a seeking of identity through wealth—dividing the property. It seems to give some identity, or rather it buys some time and some "friendship," but it neither satisfies, lasts, nor delivers what it promised. The identity sought in wealth leads into identity sought in relationships—riotous living, so the elder brother informs us. Here again, there is no answer to the cry, "Tell me who I am."

The money dries up, the friends disappear, and the end seems at hand. But truly it is the beginning, for he "comes to his senses" and starts the journey home to the One who can give him identity, meaning, significance, and self-worth.

The welcome he receives gives him the identity he sought. "This my son" says it all. The words are then reinforced by the outward symbols of celebration and affirmation, namely, the robe of sonship, the sandals of a freeman, and the ring of authority. Now he knows who he is. He has found himself in discovering the One whose service is perfect freedom.

It is a journey we all need to make—out of the hell of self-centeredness into liberation to know and be known by God, and consequently by ourselves and by others.

Breakthrough

Writing those words puts me immediately in touch with a particular crisis moment in my late teenage years. I retain a vivid awareness of the experience. It was a Sunday afternoon, and I had a deep and distressing sense of non-being, of not knowing who I was or in what way I could "find myself"—not that I could have put it in such words at the time. All I knew was that unless help was found soon I was heading for a nervous breakdown—that day. That afternoon God graciously intervened through my reading Paul Tournier's book, *The Meaning of Persons.* I was nearing the end of the book when the sentence leaped out of the page at me as a lifeline to a drowning person, or a signpost to a tired and lost traveler.

> To depend on God is to be free of men, things and self. It is to be able to take pleasure in all his gifts without being the slave of any. It is to be able, as occasion demands, to spend and to save, to speak and to forbear, to act and to rest, to be grave and gay, to defend oneself and to surrender.
>
> —Paul Tournier[4]

The sense of relief brought me to tears, to sanity, and to joy. It was a pure gift of healing truth.

Conversion

It is for this reason that I have used the word *conversion* as the theological term for "knowing." It is about turning around to face Another, and so finding our identity through a new and outer-directed awareness of God. It is a Copernican revolution, seeing Another as Center of all that is.

The picture that I have found helpful is that of the guidance system used for spacecraft. Because everything in space is moving, the earth, planets, sun, moon, and stars, it is not possible to send a command to "Go one hundred miles an hour faster," for the question is, "Faster than what?" So what happens is that the craft is "locked on" to a distant star, which is so far away that for all practical purposes it is a "fixed" star. Then, all commands sent to the spacecraft can be sent in terms of that fixed point. You can direct the craft to go faster toward, or away from, or at a prescribed angle in relation to, that fixed point. And that is the nature of our relationship to God. He is the One by whom we steer our way through life. It is in relation to him that we live out our lives.

But the best is yet to come. Once we are locked on to God, we discover that he is in active communication with us, for he is the One who has revealed himself as both Love and Word. The Cross underlines that such a Being is quite literally dying to communicate with us. Our Star is a speaking, loving, living, fixed point. We need a good receiver to accept the messages that are communicated to us. It is in this that we discover our identity and find a self to do the loving that God has called us into.

Prayer as Receiving

If we need a self to "do the loving," then prayer will involve learning to receive. This sometimes is difficult for modern people. We are more at home with prayer as achieving, getting, doing, and working—even prayer as authenticating us as "good Christians." Prayer as receiving is comparatively unknown territory. It also touches on the allergy we looked at in Chapter One. Receiving in prayer may seem strange and feel like hard work. But it is vital that we do this work, and break through the fear of being on the receiving end of love.

But how?

Essentially we do this as we learn to receive God's words of love and affirmation addressed to us. Here we run into a real barrier—our double standards. We think it thoroughly "Christian" to affirm others, to tell them they matter to God, that they are good people, pleasing to God and us. But we cannot accept that of ourselves. Equally, what we find acceptable to say about ourselves ("I'm stupid," "I'm no good," "I always get it wrong," "I'm useless"), we would consider to be thoroughly un-Christian to say, or even think, about someone else.

In other words we can celebrate another's humanity, but not our own. And this is where we need to begin, for *we are made in the image of God.* That is the starting point of Scripture and should be the starting point of our own self-acceptance. We matter to God, we are made to reflect his likeness (his personality, his ability to think, to create, to choose, and to love), and to participate in his work of creation. That "creative work" may be in building a factory, making music, or a family, school, or business. It may express itself in relationships, in "making a case" for some political issue, or simply in bringing about harmony and peace among the people whose lives we touch.

Celebrating the fact that we are made in the image of God is the beginning of our journey into wholeness. The next step is to receive, and rejoice in, the fact that *God has set his love on us through Christ.*

Prayer of the Heart

Affirming the image of God in us

Almighty God, who wonderfully created us in your own image and yet more wonderfully restored us in your Son Jesus Christ: grant that, as he came to share our human nature, so we may be partakers of his divine glory, who is alive and reigns with you and the Holy Spirit, one God, now and for ever. Amen.

—ASB; Collect for the first Sunday after Christmas

A *Story to Ponder*

The annuncation by Gabriel to Mary is an icon, or type, of the whole church. The angel addresses Mary with the words, "Greetings, you who are highly favored!" (Luke 1:28). "Hail Mary, full of grace" does not do justice to the words. The greeting is not about what Mary is, in her own right and by her own efforts; it is about who she has become because the grace, goodness, and love of God are upon her.

Mary is a symbol of the whole church. Like her we are chosen, loved, and filled with grace, by the goodness and mercy of God. Like her, the Spirit overshadows us so that Christ can be born afresh in us (Gal. 4:19). Like her, we are to respond in obedience and faith, or rather with the faith that produces the fruit of freely chosen obedience.

So we can see ourselves, like Mary, favored by God's love. Like her we need to ponder these things in our hearts and nourish our souls on the goodness of such love. We need to receive before we have anything to give.

The Cycle of Grace

Frank Lake, one of the first people to seek to integrate psychological insights with the Christian faith, developed what he called the "cycle of grace." By this he meant the way that life is intended to flow. He identified four stages.

First, we are to experience *acceptance,* simply for being who we are. If that is a regular part of our life we experience *sustenance* because we are valued. It is that which gives us our *significance,* because we matter to others and to God. Out of that grows our ability to make valued *achievements* in life.

That is very helpful. Yet even more helpful is what Frank Lake also said, namely, that our unredeemed nature tends to flow the other way around. We try to *achieve* things, so that they will give us *significance*, which will *sustain* us and enable us to *accept* ourselves. The trouble is that life will not flow that way.

In the old parsonage we used to live in, the central heating system had been added to over the years. The result was that sometimes the water went the wrong way around. When that happened the pump could not work and the whole system was dependent on gravity. The hot water went in at the bottom of the cylinder, and came out tepid. It is a picture of what happens when we do not begin our relationship with God on the basis of our acceptance in Christ.

Once we do so, grace can flow. Then we can celebrate our existence, and move on to celebrate God and the whole of creation. Rather than making us self-centered, such experience of personal worth gives us the security with which to step into the suffering of the world.

This is the good news of the gospel applied to our inner being. We need to apply it regularly to ourselves if we are to live life to the full, by grace rather than law. It is this dynamic that is expressed in the prayer exercise that follows.

Affirming the True Self

All too easily Christians take a negative view of life and of the self. After all, does not Scripture teach us to crucify the old self? Leanne Payne has written so well on this subject that I want to give her answer at this point:

> The soul, with its new center in Christ, radically changed and redirected, is to be accepted. There is the oddest thing about the history of Christian teaching. This new, real self is largely ignored, feared, or even denied. If one doubts this, he need simply run through the references in the best Bible helps. There the old or false self is catalogued and referenced in every possible way, which is absolutely good and necessary. But where is the real self acknowledged? It goes largely uncelebrated, unreferenced, and in effect unaccepted. . . . Until this redeemed self is acknowledged and accepted, we live out of the immature, unaffirmed self, and we cannot hear God aright. . . . Until we accept the new self, we are dangerous to ourselves and to others.
>
> —Leanne Payne[5]

Is this not at the root of the allergy and folly which, as we saw in the first chapter, keeps us from prayer? We fear that we will be found out by coming that close to God. Yet he comes to give life to the true self, to release the riches of his image in us. He comes to give love and to affirm our worth. If our prayer is not touched by this magnetic power of love, which draws us in, we have not yet become properly attuned to God.

This is the joyful evidence of growth in prayer—the enjoyment of God, and the personal sense of being and well-being that we receive in the process of encounter with him. It is about this that our prayer exercise is concerned. However, there is a further prayer principle to spell out, which can be of great help to us in setting the truth of God's love for us deep in our hearts.

Affirmation as Prayer

There is too much asking in prayer—especially asking for what is already ours. One way to break out of this pattern is to learn the art and place of affirmation as a way of praying.

Imagine waiting in a room to be interviewed for a new job that you are eager to get. Sitting there you are likely to be nervous. As a Christian, it is natural to turn to prayer. However, what we are likely to do is use our emotional energy to fuel prayer—but in a negative way. So we will pray something like "Lord, help me not to be anxious," "Help me not to make a fool of myself," "Please give me your peace." Valid, at one level, though each of these prayers is, what they are doing is underlining a negative in us. They are stating, in turn, that we are anxious, likely to make fools of ourselves, and lacking in peace. Yet, God has told us that he loves us, will be with us to the close of the age, and is in us.

> **Prayer Principle 4**
>
> **Affirmation Nourishes Faith**
>
> God has promised us much, and given us all things richly to enjoy. We do not have to ask for his generosity, love, and blessing—but simply receive them.
> We do that best by turning our prayers into positive affirmations of the truth.

To pray by affirmation in that situation, we simply turn the prayers into statements of the truth. "Thank you for your peace," "I receive your wisdom for this interview," "Thank you that you are with me, you are my strength," "You are Lord of my future—my times are in your hands." In this way we use our prayers to express, and so build, faith. One such affirmation we taught the whole church in my last job was:

In the multitude of Your mercies,
the greatness of Your grace,
and the power of Your Presence,
we are being made whole,
in the likeness of Christ.

Many found it a great blessing and an aid to faith—which is what prayer is meant to be. And that is particularly so when it comes to entering into God's acceptance of us. If we spend time praying "Lord, help me to accept myself," we are not likely to make progress. Such a prayer underlines to our inner being that we do not accept ourselves. Giving thanks and acting on the truth of Scripture is a richer way to pray.

Especially is the principle of the prayer of affirmation helpful when it is linked to the principle we looked at earlier of developing a liturgy of the heart. For the fact is that what we say regularly and build into our unconscious and subconscious has a powerful and formative effect on us. It shapes our thinking, behavior, and beliefs.

Prayer Exercise: Receiving the Good News into Our Hearts

- Sit down and get yourself in a comfortable position. Seek to be still, remaining silent for a minute or two. Move toward focusing on God through one or more of the following:
  - slow repetition of the two words "Our Father"
  - the words of a well-known song or hymn
  - the use of an icon or lighted candle (or you might prefer a picture of a beautiful plant or great tree, which you can use to remind yourself that good things take time grow)

  Let these means aid your faith in God's presence and his love toward you. Remember and rejoice before God that

The Spirit helps us in our weakness. We do not know what we ought to pray for, but the Spirit himself intercedes for us with groans that words cannot express (Rom. 8:26).

- Now ask God to give you good things to say to yourself that come from him.

  Below are some things we can say to ourselves, repeating them slowly a number of times:

> The God who made the universe celebrates my existence. (Alleluia)
>
> I matter to God.
>
> I am chosen and loved in Christ.
>
> I am accepted in the Beloved.

If they stir any response in you, speak that out. If not, simply keep repeating one of these truths.

I recommend that you decide beforehand how long to do it for (say, five or ten minutes) and keep to that time. This way you undermine any instinct to put yourself down for not doing it longer. In any case the more important thing is doing it regularly (preferably several times a week for several weeks).

- Remember, truth takes time to become rooted and to grow in us.
- While you may well find it helpful to start with one of the sentences above, I encourage you to expect that God will give you just the right words to speak into your heart. When that happens, rejoice—and forget my suggestions!

Yes, because we are baptized into Christ we can even say God's Word to us:

> You are my child whom I love;
>
> with you I am well pleased.

Remember that children, for their health, need affirmation about their essential worth and goodness. As children of God we also need affirmation. We have a part to play in the work of evangelism—by evangelizing (that is, proclaiming good news) to ourselves.

CHAPTER 6

Good Grief!

Encountering God through Weakness

Prayer connects us with ourselves, it is the link between our new selves that are always being transformed into God's image and our old selves with which we must come to terms if we are to be transformed.

—Roberta Bondi[1]

Healthy shame is the psycho-logical foundation of humility. It is the source of Spirituality.

—John Bradshaw[2]

Prayer is the application of the *good news* to the human heart. That is the work which was addressed in the previous chapter. But there is another side, the dark side, of human nature and experience. That also needs to be addressed in prayer. We cannot begin to address it until we have "a self to do the loving." But when we are secure in that Love, we know we can face the truth and not be overwhelmed or destroyed. This is why we considered the receiving of God's love first. Now, however, we can consider the other side, and know that we will not be rejected.

Too much prayer by Christians begins, continues, and ends in guilt. That is so tragic, for conversion is about turning from darkness to face and enter and enjoy (be enjoined to) the Light of Christ. The gospel is about liberation from guilt, not living in it. Moreover, by no means all of the darkness we need to face is our responsibility, our sin. The grief we often have to face is from the wounds we have received.

Our coming to God in this area ought not to be too difficult. Many of us first encountered God in the darkness. That darkness includes the wounds we have experienced in life, the stubborn questions that refuse to yield up answers, the hostility and injustice we experience from time to time, as well as the hostility and injustice we perpetrate on others.

How do we handle such painful issues in prayer? Essentially, it is a matter of learning to grieve well—to be in touch with our anger that results from our experience of loss, to yield to the sorrow by letting go of what is no longer an option, and then to find God's way of transcending the loss by seeing it transfigured in his purposes. That transfiguring through faith that we are led into sometimes is the strength to live with unanswered questions and know that God is there. We turn now to consider several different aspects of such good grief.

Catching the Little Foxes

In the work of farming vineyards, the children of Israel had particular problems with the little foxes. The adult ones would eat the grapes. It was frustrating, but not distressing. There were a limited number of grapes a fox could reach. It was the little foxes that had a more devastating effect, for in early spring they would eat the growing shoots of that year's branches. If the growing shoots were destroyed, the whole crop was lost, for there would be no vine on which a crop could grow. It is this trouble that forms the backdrop to the prayer of the Lover:

> Catch for us the foxes,
> the little foxes
> that ruin the vineyards,
> our vineyards that are in bloom.
>
> —Song of Songs 2:15

Notice that it is the Lover (God) addressing the Beloved (Israel). There is a vital job to do, without which there can be no fruit of intimacy between them (see John 15). It is the work of protecting the growth at its first beginnings.

For us the little foxes in our experience are the inner attitudes that eat away at the Divine affirmation of the true self that the gospel brings to us. This is what we considered in the previous chapter. All too quickly the new shoots of self-acceptance and self-worth can be destroyed. Our task is to catch those little put downs, those negative thought patterns, that would rob us of the fruit of the gospel in our lives.

We can do this best by listening to our inner dialogue and turning it up to God in prayer, seeking from him new ways of seeing ourselves and addressing our inner heart. This is no easy task, for that inner dialogue has often become so entrenched that it is a quite unconscious process going on within us and shaping the way in which we view ourselves and the world. We may never say to ourselves, "I'm no good," "I don't matter," but our lifestyle shouts it from the rooftops. Those are the little foxes we must catch.

When we have caught them, we need to bring them before God and ask him to give us words that bring life. We need to replace the inner attitude of "I don't matter," by some verse from Scripture such as:

> The LORD your God is with you,
> he is mighty to save.
> He will take great delight in you,
> he will quiet you with his love,
> he will rejoice over you with singing.
>
> —Zephaniah 3:17

It is good to personalize such Scriptures, and turn them into affirmations, by repeating to our hearts the truth that "God is with me, he is mighty to save"; "He takes delight in . . ." This work of catching the little foxes is part of listening prayer. It is something that needs to take place continually.

Dealing with the Wounds of the Past (and Present)

The little foxes of our inner dialogue usually gain entrance to our souls through wounds from deep in our past. In particular, they come from a lack of full love and affirmation from our parents or primary caregivers. We experienced love as conditional, not a gift prior to our existence, but a gift dependent on our proper performing. That proper performing may be about outward achievements that would reflect well on others, or a more inward performance of giving the emotional response that meets the needs of those on whose love we know ourselves to be totally dependent.

Dealing with these wounds involves becoming free from our parents' control and their image and expectations of us. It is no easy step, masked so often by protestations of having had a happy childhood. It may have been happy, apart from the issue that needs dealing with. Equally, what happened (good or bad) may have been described to us as "good," and we have imbibed a lie, which has shaped our view of God, life, and ourselves. Concerning these wounds, Leanne Payne writes:

> Until this redeemed self is acknowledged and accepted, we live out of the immature, unaffirmed self, and we cannot hear God aright. From that center, we also "mishear" our fellows, and they become the target of the diseased "matter" that yet resides within our souls—that is, our fear of rejection, our bitterness, envy, anger and sense of inferiority. These invariably project themselves into the minds and hearts of those we love the most, piercing them like deadly arrows.
>
> —Leanne Payne[3]

Although we can benefit from the skilled counsel of others, there is much we can do for ourselves. Remember, it is the Lover who tells the Beloved to catch the little foxes. The prayer exercise at the end of this chapter can be of great help in enabling us to name and root out wounds from the past. It involves calling sin by its name, and recognizing that we have been sinned against. We can then release that wound to the Wounded One on the Cross. Then we complete the work by releasing anyone who put that wound upon us. We do that as we speak out forgiveness of them, before God, releasing them from the debt they owe us (Matt. 18:32–33).

This is doing the work of grieving, entering into the loss of our wholeness and the pain experienced with close relationships. It is a good work that leads to life.

Making a Good Confession

We would be foolish indeed to think that all our trials are somehow "their fault." That very attitude of abdicating is a refusal to accept our responsibility for the sin that swirls around our suffering world. We need not only to learn to accept ourselves, and to forgive others, but also to confess our sins.

As I said at the beginning of this chapter, too much prayer by Christians begins, continues, and ends in guilt. The tragedy is that we do not break free at the end. We rise from prayer no less guilty, but marginally more conscious of sinfulness. We fail to enter into what Paul described as the "glorious freedom of the children of God" (Rom. 8:21). Our problem is often in discovering how to do that. Problems surface at two points: discerning true guilt and discovering true forgiveness. Let us explore these two matters further.

The first problem is that of *discerning true guilt.* The Psalmist himself knew the problem: "Who can discern his errors?" (Ps. 19:12). Remember, there are several sources of accusation against us. Other people can say "the trouble with you is . . ." or "You are unloving." We also accuse ourselves to our own hearts. The devil is described as the "accuser of our brothers, who accuses them before our God day and night" (Rev. 12:10). Indeed we know he seems especially active at night. The devil works overtime. God also accuses us, bringing us to awareness of true guilt.

The best way of discerning true guilt is to look up—to God—not in on self. The Psalmist prays:

> Search me, O God, and know my heart;
> test me and know my anxious thoughts.
> See if there is any offensive way in me,
> and lead me in the way everlasting.
>
> —Psalm 139:23–24

Notice that he does not do the searching, he leaves that to God. He seems to work on the principle of "innocent until proven guilty." Part of our diseased hearts is that we presume ourselves to be always guilty.

My experience is that false guilt is a vague feeling of being bad, rather than having done wrong, and that it makes me trapped, depressed, unable, or disinclined to take any steps. True guilt, by contrast, comes often as a shaft of light. It is frequently attached to the "way everlasting." In other words I see the way I should be going, I receive vision about right living, and that makes me aware of where I have gone wrong. It is no great effort then to change, for I have seen the light. True guilt, when joined to the work of Christ on the Cross, liberates *into* not just *from.* Watching for the *"intos"* is one of the best ways of seeing sin.

The next step is owning sin. From the Garden of Eden on, we have been incredible blameshifters. But it does not work. We cannot be rid of something which we do not admit is ours. We have to own it. Naming our sins is as vital, and life-giving, as naming our blessings. We name our blessings in order to get hold of them more firmly. We name our sins in order to let go of them more fully. So we name what is wrong, give it to God, and see him taking it into himself on the Cross.

The other thing we need to do is *discover true forgiveness.* Jesus had no doubt that celebration was the end result of recovering the lost, as the parables of the lost coin, the lost sheep, and the prodigal son make clear (Luke 15). There is celebration in each one. The angels in heaven celebrate. The woman and the shepherd celebrate. The prodigious father celebrates in no uncertain fashion. I have found it important, in confession, always to make a double confession. Whenever I confess my sins, I conclude by confessing also that Jesus is my Savior from sin. This is self-administered absolution. You do not have to be ordained to do it; the only qualification is owning your sins.

Owning Idols and Addictions

There is one further area in dealing with sin that we need to pay attention to. All too easily we see sin as "sins," specific wrong actions we have done such as being cruel or dishonest. But sin is deeper than sins. Sins are what we do. Sin is what has us. So there is an important work of recognizing the things that control us and drive us. The remarkable work of Alcoholics Anonymous has arisen out of the courage to do just that. The first step in their twelve-step recovery program is:

> We admitted we were powerless over [whatever addiction] and our lives had become unmanageable.[4]

Listening to God to bring us face to face with our idols and addictions is a very important part of both confession (of sin, rather than sins) and the work of grieving. Without it we will not be free. We will be driven people—driven by we know not what.

Addictions are not simply those associated with chemical dependence (drugs and alcohol). An addiction can be anything around which I have so organized my life that it now runs and controls me. There are "process addictions," such as the need to keep the peace, to keep everyone happy, to keep working, and to keep working on hobbies in an all-consuming way. There are also relationship addictions, "love addictions" as Pia Mellody—the author of *Facing Love Addictions* (Harper, San Francisco, '92)—calls them.

The biblical term for addictions is *idols.* Luke Johnson's definition of an idol is something I frequently come back to in my own prayer and meditation, in order to allow God to clear out any false goals and objects of "undue attention" in my life. He says:

> My god is that which
> rivets my attention,
> centers my activity,
> preoccupies my mind,
> and motivates my action.
>
> —Luke T. Johnson[5]

Put it more simply still, if you watch where your mind wanders to, when it wanders, you may well catch an idol lurking in the undergrowth of your inner life. Again, we become free of such idols when we own we have them (or, rather, that they have us), bring them before God, renounce them, and receive the gift of forgiveness and liberation.

Global Grief

Being in touch with personal grief, vulnerability, and sin makes us aware of the greater reservoir of human and global pain and injustice. Once that happens we are in a position to use that in our intercession for the world. That takes us into the final stage of grief work, namely, transcendence. Transcendence involves handling the pain in such a way that we, and the world around us, are enriched by the experience. This happens, for example, in bereavement when we incorporate into ourselves the values and characteristics of the person whose death we mourn. The person lives on in us. It happens through forgiveness, when we release others from bondage of being our debtors; we incorporate something of the heart of God by the practice of forgiveness. In this stage we are able to use the pain and brokenness of human existence to grow in our humanity and the work of compassion.

Jill Saward, a rape victim, is a fine example of someone who has experienced brutal treatment and worked through the grief to a place of transcending that pain. She formed an organization to help other rape victims. Here is the fruit of grief that can overcome evil with good.

George Hoffman, the founder of TEAR Fund—an evangelical relief agency—once said at a meeting I attended that two-thirds of those who have gone out to work on development projects in the third world are motivated by anger.

This was in no way a criticism, but rather a positive reporting. For anger can be positive energy that motivates action. Here are people in touch with the suffering of the world, who themselves are deeply touched by the injustice of the situation and are motivated to do something about it. Awareness of the injustices in the world is transformed into compassionate action.

Prayer of the Heart

The cry for help

O LORD, listen!
O LORD, forgive!
O LORD, hear and act!
For your own sake, O my God, do not delay!

—Daniel 9:19

Such transcendence begins most healthily in prayer, but will not stop when we rise from our knees. Indeed, it will direct the way we walk thereafter. So prayer and life are woven together if we are properly engaged in the work of grieving.

It is worth pointing out that here we are already in the realm of intercession and in the area of going rather than knowing. However, I raise these issues now because they do surface when we are in touch with our own grief. Moreover, I want to underline the fact that the three aspects of encountering God that form the framework of this book (seeing, knowing, and going) have soft-focus boundaries. They flow into, and out of, each other. It would be a perversion of what I am seeking to communicate to take this framework as any sort of straitjacket or technique. They are simply three aspects that are woven together in life, as in prayer.

Being and Groaning

In Romans 8, we see the process of the previous two chapters—coming into a secure sense of being, and being in touch with and working through grief—expounded in a marvelous way. First, Paul affirms the true self that emerges out of relationship to God in Christ, by the Spirit when he writes:

> For you did not receive a spirit that makes you a slave again to fear, but you received the Spirit of sonship. And by him we cry, "*Abba,* Father." The Spirit himself testifies with our spirit that we are God's children.
>
> —Romans 8:15–16

Here is the believers' security of relationship and sense of self-worth, which enable them to face and be in touch with pain and loss. Paul then goes on to speak of a threefold grieving that touches the individual, reaches out to the whole created order, and comes from the heart of God himself.

> We know that the whole creation has been groaning as in the pains of childbirth right up to the present time. Not only so, but we ourselves, who have the firstfruits of the Spirit, groan inwardly as we wait eagerly for our adoption . . . the Spirit himself intercedes for us with groans that words cannot express.
>
> —Romans 8:22, 23, 26

So the true work of grief does not turn us in on ourselves, but leads us out into the suffering of the world; as Dietrich Bonhoeffer put it, "A Christian is someone who shares the sufferings of God in the world." We will return to this again when we consider the work of intercession.

Learning Not to Fear the Dark

In all these ways, as we face our own human frailty and that of others, we can learn to handle these experiences in a way that is life-giving. When we do that we receive a bonus—the ability to encounter God and grow as people, through facing the darkness. Indeed, we come to associate difficulties, trials, and testing as doors into life.

Jacob, wrestling with an angel "until the dawn," becomes a symbol of hope for all of us wrestling with unknown forces in dark places in our lives. It is the place where growth takes place, which is why the wilderness is a symbol for encounter with God. As one of the characters in John Wyatt's book, *The Shining Levels,* says:

> You Europeans are obsessed with Things. You no longer know the meaning of simplicity. And as truth is pure simplicity you can hardly recognize it. To find truth you need to give up every Thing. Truth is brought to the world by lonely men living simply in the wilderness.
>
> —John Wyatt[6]

Character is formed in the dark. The Beatitudes point us to this truth. They begin at the place of pain, failure, and vulnerability—blessed are the poor in spirit, and blessed are those who mourn, being the first two. But they end in strength. Peacemakers become co-creators of harmony with God; this is not peacekeeping, but a richer, stronger, making of something whole that did not previously exist. They end with the strength to withstand the assaults of a hostile world—"Blessed are those who are persecuted for my name's sake." Such strength is a vulnerable, yet powerful and healing, strength. It does not control or dictate; rather it gives and it liberates. It is this holy strength of character that God gives to those with the courage and will to practice these varied aspects of good grieving.

Prayer Exercise: The Garden of the Heart

This exercise brings together the last two chapters, dealing with the affirmation of love that comes from God and the help to face the darkness within. I am indebted to Leanne Payne for this prayer exercise, the first part of which she uses to good effect in her Prayer Counseling Ministry Conferences. The second part is the natural, and balancing, progression.

Preparation

- See your life as a garden, in which there are weeds that need to be dug up.
- Be still, and take time to enter this garden; enjoy the sunlight and fragrance of its flowers.

Get in touch with its size, its layout, and the emotions of being in it.

Weeding

- See the weeds, and seek to get them out by the roots.

You will need the help of the Gardener to do a thorough and skilled job.

Remember, Mary supposed that that was what Jesus was (John 20:15).

Let him show you your part—trust him with his part.

- Take time to do a thorough job.

See if you can name the weed(s) that needs to be removed.

Seek his help if you need help in naming the issue.

- Notice what is done with the weeds after they are removed.

Reflect on the experience (do not rush it, or step too quickly out of it into "analysis").

What does the experience tell you about what God wants to root out of your life? Note your response to this weeding. Is it eager, anxious, relieved, or what?

- Note any way that it speaks to you: Put it down in your prayer journal.

Planting

- Now comes the planting of new plants for future flowering ("love, joy, peace—like flowers—spring in his path to birth").

Enjoy this good experience.

Imagine the pleasure and peace and enjoyment of filling the garden with color.

- Notice the smallest plants (the alpines) and the sturdy bushes. They all have a place.
- Notice what is there: you are not starting from scratch. Good plants already bloom there.

Be aware of the ways you and the Gardener are working together. Name the plants—what do they symbolize in your life?

Ask for help in naming the plants if you need it.

Stand back and enjoy what has been planted; imagine the growth in one or two months' or one or two years' time. Enjoy it with him.

- What does the experience tell you that God is wanting to plant in your life?
    - Make a note of every aspect of the experience which speaks to you.

Chapter 7

Praying Back the Scriptures

Encountering God through Bible Meditation

The word of God is a special sacrament of his presence, just as real, although different in form, as his presence in the Eucharist.

—Gerard Hughes[1]

The first principle in beginning to listen to God is that of taking the sacred texts into our very spirits and souls by prayerful meditation upon them. His word then "abides in us," burning as an inner light, and we cry out to God. This is oratio, responsive speech born of God's word aflame within.

—Leanne Payne[2]

Notwithstanding Thomas Cranmer's masterly crafting of the Church of England's Book of Common Prayer, and the work in our own day of the Liturgical Commission of the Church of England, the Bible is *the* Christian's Prayer Book. It is our greatest source of prayer and our great resource in praying.

Indeed, prayer and Scripture are rather like the oxygen and hydrogen which, when mixed together, ignite and create liftoff for the space shuttle and other rockets. The power of these two sources of energy, prayer and the reading of Scripture, can truly lift us into the heavens. Too often Christians have these two resources in separate sealed containers with no means of mixing.

This chapter is about "mixing it" in prayer! It is about how to harness the power of God's Word to our prayer life. The mixing is not just of Scripture and our prayers, but of Scripture and our lives. Prayer is simply the mixer, the means of joining life and truth. How does it happen?

Our knowing of God comes to us in large measure through our encounter with him in meditation on Scripture. God's Word is creative energy. By a word God created the whole universe. By his living Word, Jesus Christ, he has redeemed the whole of that creation, bringing it back within his eternal purposes. He now comes to us, between creation and the consummation of the ages, to continue his work in the process of new creation within and through the believer. God does so by speaking his Word into our lives, to bring his likeness into being and to give us a foretaste of the fulfillment to come.

Truly to hear, and in listening to obey, is at the heart of knowing God.

That knowing is itself a gift of God. It points to the double source of the inspiration of Scripture. God not only breathed life and truth into those who wrote, by which they become a living word to us, but he now breathes life into the hearers of his Word, by which we become alive with the truth of God.

I had a striking experience of this on the very first day of my being a Christian. After making a commitment to Christ on Easter Eve, as a teenager, I went to bed thinking the whole thing had been a waste of time. I felt no different. Yet, the next morning, the whole world seemed different. Easter Day really was "a Passover of gladness, a Passover of God."

In the afternoon, the person who had brought me to faith spent half an hour showing me verses in the Bible which explained what it means to be a Christian and to live by faith in God. Until the day before, I had rated the Bible the most boring book in the world—well actually, it was equally top (or bottom?!) with Shakespeare. However, that day it came alive to me, and spoke as if it were personally addressed only to me. It was no longer a school textbook. It was more like a love letter—intimate, affirming, understanding, and speaking with deep empathy into my experience of life.

True Knowing

This knowing and being known takes place when God's Word so penetrates our innermost being that we become what we hear. We are transformed into God's likeness.

The importance of listening as the key to knowing is underlined by Old and New Testaments alike. The listening that is meant is a deep hearing of the inner heart which is transformed by that hearing. This is how intimacy with God takes place. We know by hearing. Significantly, it was the lack of true hearing that was God's chief complaint against the false prophets:

> If they had stood in my council, they would have proclaimed my words to my people and would have turned them from their evil ways and from their evil deeds.
>
> —Jeremiah 23:22

The contrast with the Servant of the Lord, in Isaiah, is striking. Of him we read:

> The Sovereign LORD has given me an instructed tongue,
>   to know the word that sustains the weary.
> He wakens me morning by morning,
>   wakens my ear to listen like one being taught.
> The Sovereign LORD has opened my ears,
>   and I have not been rebellious.
>
> —Isaiah 50:4–5

Jesus continually urged his disciples to listen at this level with the whole of their being: "He who has ears to hear, let him hear" (Matt. 11:15; 13:9–17, 43). How then can we listen "with our whole heart" so that we may be transformed from one degree of glory to another? For this is the purpose of our knowing and being known by God.

Personal Dialogue

The key to such prayer lies in establishing a dialogue between ourselves and God. One particular principle has been vital in my own experience of prayer. It is a principle we will be returning to repeatedly in the remaining chapters of the book.

It is encapsulated in the, at first sight, puzzling phrase "liturgical sentence and charismatic response." That may not be enlightening by itself, so let me explain. What I mean is that there is both a set ("fixed") part of prayer and a spontaneous ("free") part. It is an enormous help in our prayer life if we can develop a rhythm of speaking out a liturgical sentence (a set verse of Scripture or part of a hymn or prayer), and then express our own response in our own words (that is what I mean by charismatic response).

> **Prayer Principle 5**
>
> **Structure Your Prayer into Sentence and Response**
>
> Using a set text—whether Scripture, poetry, hymn, or prayer—and making our own spontaneous response into an expression of prayer liberates us from undue responsibility for prayer being wholly dependent on us.

So, for example, we can use a well-known verse such as "God so loved the world"; as we meditate on it, we make response to God. We thank him that he does love the world, or we can ask him to enable us to love the world as Jesus did, or pray that the world he has made will discover and experience that love.

This a very simple, easy-to-remember way of meditating on Scripture. Moreover, it applies to practically the whole of Scripture. Almost any verse can draw out of us a response of prayer or worship. All we need to do is to read a phrase, sentence, or verse from Scripture and then respond to God from within that verse.

At the end of this chapter is an exercise designed to help us take God's Word into our lives in this way. It is an approach that Colin Urquhart develops throughout the whole of his book *In Christ Jesus,* and outlines particularly on page 93.

The Seed of the Word

The purpose of praying back the Scriptures is to take them to heart—to take them into our hearts, our innermost nature, so that we are shaped by what we hear. The cynic has said of humanity that "we are what we eat." The Christian, feeding alike on God's Word and the sacrament of communion, can say "Amen" to that—not out of cynicism, but by faith.

The harvest analogy, seen most clearly in the parable of the sower, expresses this truth about the seed of God's Word being planted in our lives. It tells us that "the one who sowed the good seed is the Son of Man" (Matt. 13:37). God's Word is like a seed planted in us which is to grow to maturity (1 Peter 1:23–25). Praying back the Scriptures is the way both to plant and to water that seed (Isa. 61:3). The same imagery lies behind the picture of the Vine and the branches in John 15.

This way of handling Scripture is far from new. It is part of the history of spiritual life in all the traditions of the church. The importance of hiding God's Word in our heart (Ps. 119:11) is rooted first of all in Scripture itself. Joshua is told to "meditate on the Law day and night." Mary "pondered all these things in her heart," and Jesus clearly meditated on God's Word throughout his life, and drew the appropriate truths out of his storehouse of wisdom as the situation required.

The monastic movement was a renewal movement fired by hunger for God's Word. Particularly with few written copies of the Scriptures available, writing God's Word "on the heart" was about the only place most people could afford to write it. The Navigator movement was built largely on the foundation of memorizing Scripture. Jean Darnell, a fine American Pentecostal pastor who worked in the United Kingdom for several decades, used to give people whom she counseled a "Scripture prescription," which was to be "repeated three times daily after meals"!

I think of a young mother who was struggling in her relationship with her eldest child, and went to her pastor to ask for help—specifically for a verse. He gave her Romans 5:5, "God has poured out his love into our hearts by the Holy Spirit, whom he has given us." This mother did not so much hide it in her heart, as clung to it desperately as if it were a rope attached to a liferaft. She can see, looking back, that it was indeed a lifeline. It kept her afloat, built in her confidence in what God could do. Notice it is God who *has* already shed abroad his love, by the Holy Spirit who *has* been given to us. It was an inspired text to give, because it did not tell her anything that she ought to do or be, but simply stated and affirmed what God had already done.

Entering the Story

So far we have thought about a single phrase, sentence, or verse of Scripture entering into us and becoming rooted and growing to shape our character and actions. This is the picture that Paul holds out to us in such faith-building words in 2 Corinthians. He had been speaking about a veil being over the eyes of the Israelites when the Old Covenant is read. He then goes on to say:

> But whenever anyone turns to the Lord, the veil is taken away. Now the Lord is the Spirit, and where the Spirit of the Lord is, there is freedom. And we, who with unveiled faces all reflect the Lord's glory, are being transformed into his likeness with ever-increasing glory, which comes from the Lord, who is the Spirit.
>
> —2 Corinthians 3:16–18

However, there is another way in which we can see and read Scripture. Rather than taking a verse into ourselves, we can step into a whole story. This is at the heart of Ignatian spirituality. It involves using the imagination and finding ourselves in the story.

As we saw back in Chapter Two ("An Open Door"), stories are very important to us all in helping us find our place in life. Jews find their identity as the exodus community, and Christians are held together—despite many and often trivial differences—by the Jesus story. Families (and churches) have stories that shape their identity. The two communities in Northern Ireland find their identity in two different stories that go back hundreds of years, as do the warring factions in the former state of Yugoslavia. This is why the problems are so difficult to deal with. It is the stories that must be addressed, not just—or primarily—the points on which there is disagreement.

We know how important stories are for children, and what security and peace they experience when a story is read to them over and over again. It touches their souls, for stories are a powerful means of finding our identity.

There are many different temperaments among people, but in many ways we tend to connect with reality most easily either by thinking (having rational thoughts in verbal form), or through our feelings (we see life through the varied hues of our many different emotions), or by action (using our six senses to find our way through life), or by intuition (our instincts and our "feel" for what is possible, right, or true). It helps to know how we most easily relate to life. It will affect how we pray. Remember, we all function in all these ways, it is just a matter of knowing which is the main road into our inner life. In prayer it is good to start with that approach, and then to seek to develop also the other avenues into "knowing."

With that in mind we can read a story and enter it through our imagination, trying to picture the color of the trees that Jonah sat under, the scale of the waters that were held back when the Israelites crossed the Red Sea, the feelings of the shepherds on the way to Bethlehem, the arguments Pilate's wife might have used to get him to hand Jesus over, and so on.

As we do this we will find ourselves addressed by the story. I led a group once through Joshua's experience before the battle of Jericho (Josh. 5:13–15). When I asked people afterwards to share what they had experienced, one person brought up the question, "What are the sandals I should be taking off?" Interestingly the answer was not clear, but the fact that the question mattered in a believer's relationship with God was. This is a reminder of the prayer principle of sowing and reaping. Knowing and being known do not always, or normally, yield to instant answers. Staying with unanswered questions is an important way of listening to God.

There is a prayer exercise at the end of this chapter that is intended to help in "entering the story of Scripture." Melvyn Matthew's book, *The Hidden Word,* is a helpful aid to this way of relating to Scripture.

One way in which this whole aspect of knowing God was opened up for me happened when I decided to read the parable of the prodigal son as my only reading of Scripture for a month. Initially it was, quite frankly, boring. I knew it so well, I could hardly keep my eyes on the page and read the words. But after about the fourth day I saw something I had not seen before. That happened again the next day, and most days. I ended the month "entering into" the story of the prodigal son with a sense of enthusiasm and anticipation.

Conclusion

We have considered two ways in which we can harness Scripture to our prayer life. One is by planting seeds of God's Word in our hearts. They will be bite-sized portions that we can digest and "chew over." The other is by immersing ourselves in the stories of Scripture and finding ourselves in them. There are two exercises below which are expressions of these two ways of entering Scripture and allowing it to enter us. Once you have become familiar with these specific exercises, they should enable you to take almost any text or story in Scripture and through it to strengthen prayer as a means of encountering God.

Prayer Exercise 1: Receiving the Seed of God's Word

Choose a verse of Scripture that you want to see planted and bearing fruit in your life—here are three contrasting possibilities, but much of Scripture can be handled in this way:

- "Take off your sandals, for the place where you are standing is holy ground."

(for seeing the presence of God and the presence of the holy in the whole of life)

- "Come down immediately. I must stay at your house today."

(to grasp the wonder of the humanity of Christ as seen in his befriending of Zacchaeus)

- "God has poured out his love into our hearts by the Holy Spirit, whom he has given us."

(to be shaped and filled by the love revealed to us in the actions, character, and heart of God)

- Sit down and relax. With hands open upwards in an attitude of faith and receiving, focus first on God—his presence with you and his love toward you.
- Then recite the verse slowly several times (half a dozen or more). Repeat the Scripture slowly. Say it with faith, receiving it into your being.
- Pause between repetitions, a little longer each time. If a response comes to mind, speak it out. It may be a simple "Thank you, Jesus" or something longer. Do not ramble on: A sentence or two is enough. The moment you feel as if you are "drying up," repeat the verse.

It is good to decide beforehand how long you are going to do this for—say, five or ten minutes—then keep to that, and do it regularly, using the same verse for several weeks at a time.

The important principle is not to strive. If you have no spontaneous response, flow back into repeating the Scripture. If you spend ten minutes slowly repeating and receiving the Scripture, you will have ministered the truth into your inner being.

If you have a response, then express it; if you do not, continue repeating the Scripture.

In this way you take the truth into yourself: You plant the seed of the Word in your life. You plant the acorn. God promises that "they will be called oaks of righteousness, a planting of the Lord, for the display of his splendor" (Isa. 61:3).

Prayer Exercise 2: Entering the Story of Scripture

To aid this exercise the story is printed here. It is from Mark 10:46–52.

> Then they came to Jericho. As Jesus and his disciples, together with a large crowd, were leaving the city, a blind man, Bartimaeus (that is, the Son of Timaeus), was sitting by the roadside begging. When he heard that it was Jesus of Nazareth, he began to shout, "Jesus, Son of David, have mercy on me!"
>
> Many rebuked him and told him to be quiet, but he shouted all the more, "Son of David, have mercy on me!"
>
> Jesus stopped and said, "Call him."
>
> So they called to the blind man, "Cheer up! On your feet! He's calling you."
>
> Throwing his cloak aside, he jumped to his feet and came to Jesus.
>
> "What do you want me to do for you?" Jesus asked him.
>
> The blind man said, "Rabbi, I want to see."
>
> "Go," said Jesus, "your faith has healed you." Immediately he received his sight and followed Jesus along the road.

- Enter this story in your imagination.
  - Mingle with the crowd, sense the heat of the day, the swirling dust, the growing tiredness, and maybe irritability of those following Jesus that day.
  - Be one of the first to catch sight of Bartimaeus; notice your reactions.

- Watch the disciples (like bouncers) trying to keep some order in the place.
    - Imagine what they might be saying to each other or to Bartimaeus.
    - Notice your feelings as the story develops.
    - Take time to see yourself as a disciple.
    - Let their understandable, but un-kingdom like response challenge your excuses about it being "not appropriate" to live by the values of the age to come.
- Feel the whole story from Bartimaeus's perspective:
    - the long years of despair and frustration
    - the quickening spark of hope based on stories he would have heard
    - the courage and desperation behind his full-throated shout for help
    - his total disinterest in respectability and social propriety—if he could be healed

    Let yourself be Bartimaeus. Cry out to God for the healing you need.

- Watch Jesus
    - his availability, awareness, compassion, authority
- Respond to the whole event with:
    - praise to Jesus for who he is and what he does and
    - trusting openness to his power to break into the difficult parts of your life—like Bartimaeus

CHAPTER 8

Listening Prayer

Encountering God Within

Our specifically human existence consists precisely in our hearing the Word of God. We are what we hear from God.

—Emil Brunner[1]

Who can ever master something in which the main object is to be mastered?

—Richard Foster[2]

It has not been easy to resist the urge, at the start of each chapter, to say "this is the heart of prayer," or "this is the most important part of this book." I will continue to resist that temptation because there are other equally important aspects of prayer to come. However, it can certainly be said that this is the least practiced or appreciated dimension of prayer. "Prayer" for most people, and probably for most Christians, is about talking *to* God, *telling* him about our needs, and—if we could but see it—*giving* him the benefit of our wisdom and advice. In church situations, where people come forward at the end of a service or meeting to be prayed for, I have found time and time again that so many are as eager to tell God their needs as they are deaf to any idea that they might get an answer. As some people have poured out their heart to God, with me alongside them, they have finished what they have to say, and gotten up to walk away. I have often had to say, "How about waiting for an answer?" The truth is that the more important part of prayer is what God says to us, how he shapes and directs us.

The previous three chapters in particular have prepared us for this stage in prayer. We have already engaged with listening prayer in those chapters, doing some important groundwork. We cannot hear God aright unless there is some degree of self-acceptance and affirmation of who I am as a new creation in Christ. Without that first step, there is nowhere for the seed of the Word to be planted. Equally, unless we are in touch with the old "diseased self," and the distortions it brings to our whole way of seeing life, God, and particularly ourselves, we will be poor receivers of what God is saying to us. Moreover, unless our hearing from God is rooted in relationship to him through Scripture, we will be at the mercy of every whim or fad or notion—and take them for the voice of God.

So what more is there to listening prayer than has already been considered?

Living in Response to God

The first thing to underline is that to be a disciple is to be someone who has chosen to live life in response to what

God is saying to us. This is where the idea of life as a journey or pilgrimage is so helpful. Too often we settle down (as Abraham and his father had done before God's call came to Abraham—see Gen. 11:31b) and think we have arrived. You hardly need any instruction if that is the case. You have life sorted out, there is nothing to do but "live happily ever after." If, however, you see life as a journey, then you will continually need to lok at the map, consider which fork in the road to choose, and consult the best guide available. Listening prayer has that sense of journey about it. It is the practice of what King David was continually reported as doing, namely, "inquiring of the Lord."

This is the heart of conversion. It is a turning around from running and directing my own life, to living in response to God's call, choosing his Word and his Way. Indeed the word *listen* means "to obey," because it has about it that quality of listening that takes what is said "to heart," and acts on it.

Jesus Our Model

We see in the life of Jesus a wonderful example of what it means to live by listening, to live in response to God's call upon our lives. It is evident in two particular ways: how he began his ministry and how he continued it.

The ministry of Jesus began in his baptism, in the course of which he heard the Father addressing him in these words: "You are my Son, whom I love; with you I am well pleased" (Luke 3:22). Notice that he heard the Father address him through the words of Scripture. This is why learning to pray back the Scriptures is so vital to the work of listening prayer. It is often in the act of praying them back that they reach down and take hold of us, becoming God's living Word to us.

Notice also that the Word came to Jesus on two levels. First, there was powerful personal affirmation. To be assured of relationship to God, and security in his totally accepting love, is good news indeed. The great "I am's" of John's Gospel grew in the fertile soil of such acceptance by his heavenly Father. So many of the voices we hear, and allow into our hearts to shape our actions, are destructive of that foundation of self-worth before God. As John Bradshaw puts it:

> Jesus said: "Before Abraham was, I AM." They crucified him for this. The old order crucifies all of us for expressing our "I-amness" and creativity.

We must train our hearts to listen to the affirming word. It is foundational to our very being. We are "becoming people," people in a lifelong process of becoming who we are. That becoming happens in response to others. We are called into being. We do not find it within, but by being addressed by one who loves, accepts, affirms, and mirrors back to us our true self. This is what God does in prayer—if we will dare to listen. First, then, we can expect to hear words of personal affirmation.

But there was another side to the voice that spoke to Jesus. The affirming word strengthened his sense of being; yet hidden within that word was a call into mission. The "word from the Father" was an amalgam of two Old Testament Scriptures: one about David's royal reign (Ps. 2:7), and the other taken from the song of the Suffering Servant (Isa. 42:1). No one before had put together kingship and suffering. That word became the agenda for the whole life and mission of Jesus—to bring in the kingdom of God by way of suffering love. Notice here, as we saw in Chapter Two, that this encounter with God was not just for that particular moment, but for the whole of his life. How important it is for us to listen and draw strength and direction from our encounters with God.

We too, then, are to expect God to both affirm our sense of worth before him and give us directions for ordering our lives around the coming of his kingdom and the doing of his will.

Jesus, the One Who Listened

Although Jesus is spoken of in Scripture as the Word of God and the Word-made-flesh, it is also true that in revealing true humanity to us, he has shown that it consists of a continual process of listening to God. To be human is to be a Word-receiving being. A vital part of that process is an eagerness and determination to listen. The following Scriptures show how this theme of life as a response to the Word which God addresses to us, was central to who Jesus was, as well as to what he did:

> "Man does not live on bread alone, but on every word that comes from the mouth of God . . ."
>
> —Matthew 4:4

> "My mother and brothers are those who hear God's word and put it into practice . . ."
>
> —Luke 8:21

> "My food," said Jesus, "is to do the will of him who sent me and to finish his work . . ."
>
> —John 4:34

> "I tell you the truth, the Son can do nothing by himself; he can do only what he sees his Father doing, because whatever the Father does the Son also does . . ."
>
> —John 5:19

All that Jesus says about "his hour" is part of this process of not taking the law, or life, into his own hands, but listening to the leading and directing of the Father.

In summary, in the life of Jesus we see that his primary encounter with the Father addressed both his being and his doing, and that this became foundational to his whole living. He first listened to the word the Father was addressing to him, and then acted accordingly. If this was true of Jesus then it must be vital for us as his followers, to be in the company of those who listen to God. How is it to be done? I want to answer that question by speaking first from personal experience, and then spelling out some basic principles.

Part of My Journey

When the time came to leave a parish after over twenty years, I moved from sensing God putting the thought of a move into my mind, to having that confirmed, finding the right move, and beginning to settle into a new work. As I look back I can see that God has spoken in a number of ways.

It probably began in the *emotions* as a certain loss of motivation. There were difficult tasks and great challenges in the life of the church, and nothing seemed straightforward, nor did my insights immediately win the day or the argument. That was no different from the previous twenty years in the same job. What was different was a lack of energy to find a way through. So my listening began by listening to my feelings—before God. Did I need a break, was I working too hard, had I lost my first love? These questions naturally came to the fore, although I had already discovered that just because an idea is based on a critical view of oneself, does not mean that it is what God is saying. Nor is the opposite true.

What happened cut right across all that thinking with a *"word from God"* that was very specific: "This work has been a fruitful field, but now the time has come to plow it up for the next harvest, and you are to have no part in that." It is difficult to get clearer marching orders! How did that word come? I can only say that one day it was there. (I have often found that a word from God is suddenly there.) I never saw it coming. Keeping a journal was almost certainly crucial to my catching the word when it came, since my experience is that God's Word comes more like a butterfly on the shoulder than a thunderbolt on the head.

There followed a long period (at least, it felt like that at the time!) of *silence.* I was seeking a move, with little or nothing coming. One or two possibilities appeared on the horizon. With some of them I convinced myself that this was it, only to see them disappear back over the horizon. This created a wilderness sensation, a lack of hearing from God—or anyone. But God speaks in and through the silence. He makes himself known by his absence. That divine withdrawal led to a vital time of personal growth in which I had to address feelings of self-pity (disguised pride), and come to a fuller sense of acceptance before God for who I am, rather than what I do. Dark and difficult though it was, it was a time of giving and blessing.

I was sustained in that by two verses that leaped out of the pages of *Scripture* at me. The first was, "the LORD delights in those who fear him, who put their hope in his unfailing love" (Ps. 147:11). It was followed a few weeks later by my sensing the description of Abraham as God's call on my life. The writer to the Hebrews says he "went, even though he did not know where he was going" (Heb. 11:8). As I continued to listen before God I became aware that he was separating me from my identity as a clergyman—to be a person, not just a parson.

Two further elements contributed to the completion of this process. First, the prayer of friends, who had some *pictures* that related to how my present job appeared. It kept on coming back—despite some serious evasive action on my part. The picture was of a film being developed. Film must be dipped into developing solution again and again, until the picture is clear. That was what was happening with this particular possibility.

The final stage was a sense of *call from the church.* I had often said that while the church today tests the "call" of those putting themselves forward for ordination, the New Testament suggests a pattern of the church working the other way round. The church then seems rather to have done the calling into ministry. Now I was experiencing it firsthand, for it was what leaders in the church were saying to me about my suitability for the work, not what I felt, that constituted the call.

Drawing Some Lessons

I have told this story in some detail as often stories tell more than bare principles. My experience underlined to me that listening is a way of life, and that God speaks in "many and varied" ways—through Scripture, by a direct word from him, through others, in experience, through dreams, and through silence. All have a part to play. Keeping a journal has proved crucial to listening; otherwise what is being said disappears like a morning mist.

However, this is a story of listening at the easier end of the spectrum of life, namely, about an outward issue of a job and a move. The other end of the spectrum—listening to God about my own journey into growth as a person—is more important and more elusive although the two are bound together. It is this moving forward in personal growth that is vital to life and to true discipleship.

It is about this aspect of listening that I want to identify some ways that are important. But first let me answer the question that is sometimes raised at this point, namely, "How do you set about listening?" The basic answer is to make time to be quiet and unhurried. Simply being still with nothing else to do and no deadline to meet is what is needed to listen. The question is, do I make time for such prayer, or is my prayer all busy and "getting on" prayers?

Prayer of the Heart
Calming our hearts to listen

Calm me O Lord
as you stilled the storm
Still me O Lord,
keep me from harm
Let all the tumult
within me cease
Enfold me Lord in your peace.

—From David Adam,
The Edge of Glory

Although I have sometimes spent a whole day at a time, my more usual listening prayer is done over a half to three-quarters of an hour period. The most difficult part is simply to make the time and to give it priority. The next step, and next most difficult part, is to still my heart and turn my thoughts to God. The exercise at the end of Chapter One on "letting go" is a great help in slowing the pace down and enabling me to be on God's wavelength; indeed, I find it helpful to see myself as a radio receiver being tuned in to the eternal frequency of truth and love. The listening then often has three stages. They are not neat and tidy compartments and I do not always major on all three, but they are three elements that are important in listening.

Stage One: Listen to Life

This is the obvious starting point: to reflect on, and listen to, what life has been saying to us—or rather what God has been saying to us through life. Included in this are several elements.

Listening to our experience of life. Reviewing what has been happening to us, and the events that define our life at present, is an obvious place to begin. The important thing is to seek to discern what God is saying to us through those experiences; as Neville Ward[3] has put it:

> every experience is a kind of annunciation.

The natural instinct is to review our experience with a view to blaming others and proving ourselves right. Before Love, which accepts us fully, we can however dare to listen to the fuller picture. In particular we are to seek to discern what God is saying to us. Sometimes he is calling us to trust him with the unknown, and at other times he is calling us to rise up and resist the evil or injustice that confronts us or others. Not infrequently I have felt a sense of "here we go again," as a repeated pattern emerges. It is important to listen to such patterns because they often tell us what we are reluctant to face and find a way through. Having considered what is happening, it is important to go on to ask why this is happening to me, and more important still, what God is saying through this experience.

Listening to our motivation. Often God is wanting us to see the true motivation for our actions. He does this, not in order to blame us, but rather to set us free from being driven, rather than called people. Am I continually overworking, getting into debt, losing my temper, being put down at work, or whatever? When we have identified a repeated pattern, we can then bring it to God in prayer and seek the gift of interpretation. It does not always come immediately, not because God has a problem thinking up an answer, but because we have a problem hearing answers.

Listening to our emotions. All too easily we project unacknowledged feelings onto other people. Before God we can dare to own those feelings and discern what we are to do about them. Only when we are honest about them can we handle them well and have some confidence that they are informing rather than distorting our judgment. The process involves getting in touch with what we feel, and then naming it. Just like Adam naming the animals, and thereby giving them their identity, we need to do the same with our feelings.

We then apply our minds to consider why we are feeling this way, and can go on—before God—to choose the right response. It may be to "have it out with someone," or to forgive another person, to choose to do something, or to await God's timing. It is that choosing of the response before God that enables us to hear. Remember, we are called upon to overcome evil with good. Listening to our emotions enables us to shift into a more creative gear than retaliation. It equips us to respond to life, rather than react to it.

Stage Two: Listening to Desires

Stage one is about listening in a reactive, albeit creative, way to what is happening to us. This next stage involves our participating with God in shaping life. Jesus said that he came to give us life "in all its abundance." There are hopes, desires, and hidden energies and vitality in all of us. Listening prayer is a way of mining those resources.

We are often inhibited in this work because of a low self-image, and because we feel that somehow Christians should have no will of their own. The opposite is the truth. God wants us to be fully human, fully alive. That means having a strong and healthy will—harnessed to God's will ("your kingdom come, your will be done"). Here are two people who have much to teach us in this matter of getting in touch with these deepest desires within us.

> Desire, in my opinion, is among the most important of these radiant things that must be allowed to surface. . . . It takes the real self to truly desire, and in its desiring all that is good, beautiful, and true, it more quickly and wonderfully functions in the image of its Maker.
>
> —Leanne Payne[4]

> If we were able to discover what we really want, if we could become conscious of the deepest desire within us, then we should have discovered God's will. . . . The saint is the person who has discovered his/her deepest desire. They then "do their own thing," which is also God's thing.
>
> —Gerard Hughes[5]

To be in touch with desire is to be in touch with life from Above—within. It is no easy task, for desire is easily buried by the pressures of living, the fear of failure, and the loss of the true self. In seeking to reconnect with them we may well discover how the true self has been put to death and needs awakening. But in this pursuit, life breaks forth—resurrection, new creation. In a culture that has harnessed desire to false gods and unhealed emotions, and now lacks joy, and hope, desire is also needed for our survival as a people. Truly, as James Houston puts it, "The absence of desire can kill prayer."[6]

Stage Three: Listening for the Divine Word

In listening to life, and to desire, we listen to God. Yet there is a specific, focused listening to God which is also to take place. We are to wait before God for him to address us. It may well be a word that comes through and in our listening to life and to desire. But there is also simply a holding of ourselves before God for him to speak truth, life, and light into our souls.

Often this comes, particularly initially, in seemingly banal form which we hesitate to share with others. We are not to despise the day of small things if they speak to us and touch our heart. "I love you," "You are special to me," are not to be dismissed, but received, and cherished. Out of them will grow richer, stronger words that renew our inner life, sharpen our hearing. In this address by God we also encounter the "easy yoke" of which Jesus spoke, the being joined to him, which sets us free from diseased attitudes within and false pressures without. It is indeed the life-giving Word that nourishes the soul. It comes to those who hold themselves before God with openness to all that he desires to give them.

Prayer Exercise: Listening

With paper, or prayer journal, and pen, set aside ten, twenty, or thirty minutes to listen to God. It is best to start with just ten minutes, and build from there. Do not be discouraged if you feel you hear nothing to begin with. Remember, although you cannot recall how many steps you took before you learned to walk, you know it was a skill worth developing even if it took a thousand failures.

- Prepare yourself with two minutes of letting go and receiving from God.

  You may well find that there are, in practice, three distinct exercises in this one exercise. Simply get as far as you can in your time frame. Not having enough time is a good thing; it spurs us on to come back and listen again.

Listening to Life

Reflect on your recent experience of life.

- What are the major events?
- What have been the dominant emotions?

- What is life "calling out of you"?
- What response do you sense God is calling you to make?

Listening to Desires

You may have to go back many years to get in touch with hopes and dreams and desires. From the last such time you can recall, work forward, and recall any moments of longing . . . elation . . . joy . . . hope . . . harmony . . .

- See them as God's gifts to you on your journey of faith.
- Ask him to show you how to hold on to those moments and draw strength from them.
- Ask for insight to see how they, rather than events around you, should shape your life and your priorities.

Listening to God

Give thanks to God for his life in you and his love for you. Be still, turn your head and hands and thoughts up to God in openness.

- Simply ask him to speak to you.
- Write down what comes to mind.
- Do not try to hear so much as focus on him—the Word comes most easily in the embrace of the Beloved.

Receive every gift with thanksgiving, noting it and pondering it in your heart.

Part 4

GOING

CHAPTER 9

Intercession

Encountering God in Prayer for Others

> Prayer is a way of life which begins and ends in love.
>
> —Roberta Bondi[1]

> We are called to be physicians of that civilization about which we dream, the civilization of love.
>
> —Pope Paul VI, December 31, 1975

The third stage in the journey of prayer, after we have entered into *seeing* the wonder of God, and following on from the process of *knowing* God and being changed into his likeness, is our *going* out "to live and work to your praise and glory," as the Anglican liturgy puts it.

This going has two distinct stages. First we "go" in prayer, and then we are to "go" in action, although—as we shall see in the chapter "Practicing the Presence of God"—we never go from God's presence. Rather, that second stage of going is a going with and into his presence: "Surely I am with you always, to the very end of the age" (Matt. 28:20). In the next two chapters we will consider how we are to "go" in prayer, that is, how we are to turn our thoughts out to the world around us and, in intercession, give attention to the needs of the world. In doing so, we fulfill the second great commandment, to love others. The final two chapters will then consider how we go in action and retain awareness of the reality of God's presence and action in our lives.

There is a real danger, particularly in the me-centered culture in which we live, that we never do break out from self-concern in prayer. It is this that makes intercession seem like hard work. It is also one reason why we need to pray for the world—so that we might be liberated from self-concern. Richard Lovelace writes about those who are

> so tied up in programs of spiritual self-improvement that they have no time to care about anything but the throbbing self-concern at the center of their consciousness. . . .

He reminds us rather that

> radical faith in Christ frees the Christian from spiritual self-concern to give attention to God and others, and to think and pray about the reformation of structures.
>
> —Richard Lovelace[2]

Having explored earlier how to use Scripture as a resource for prayer, I want now to continue that theme, by looking at intercession from the starting point of praying back the prayers of Scripture. What I am proposing is that we see the prayers in Scripture as the fertile soil out of which intercession can grow. Once we have such soil we can then plant out our own particular flowers of prayer for the needs of others.

The Art of Sensible Praying

I do not mean to use the word *sensible* in the way we immediately think of it—the parental admonition to be reasonable and not cause anyone trouble. I use it rather in the more creative and enriching sense of praying with our senses, not least in touch with our emotions. Prayer is to be wholehearted, that is, done with the whole heart. And with the body too.

We have so much to learn from Jewish traditions of prayer. Their most famous place of prayer is the Wailing Wall. It must be difficult to pray there if your prayer is all in the mind, and you are not in touch with your feelings. For emotions are a vast resource for prayer; they can energize prayers of grief, compassion, anger, and justice. As we pray for the world it will greatly enrich our praying if we make contact with our emotions and pray with passion (literally: strong feelings).

Our bodies are also a great prayer resource. Again, the normal Jewish physical posture is most instructive. It is one of standing, with head raised looking up to heaven and hands open wide, expressive of openness and vulnerability. It is a posture that expresses full confidence in how we will be received by the One to whom we make ourselves vulnerable.

> **Prayer Principle 6**
>
> **Pray with "Attitude"**
>
> Prayer is not just a matter of words; it engages with every part of us. We need to develop the use of our emotions, imagination, intuition, and senses. We can then learn to pray through our attitude, even without formulating words.

In contrast, the normal Western Christian posture for prayer is seated, head bowed (in shame?), eyes closed (in case we see the world?), and head clasped in the hands (lest we hear anything?). As a grief posture it is quite appropriate; but there is more to prayer than grief. What is more, I suspect that the grief being expressed is about ourselves ("I am a worm and not a man," Ps. 22:6) and lack of self-acceptance, rather than any sense of entering into the pain and anguish of the world.

In this connection I notice an interesting contrast between what Jesus did and what he taught. He taught us, in prayer, to "go into your room, close the door and pray" (Matt. 6:6), whereas what he did was to go into the desert and hills. There is a place for both, and some may not have access to their own space (although that may be rare today), while others do not have ready access to the countryside. However, even in a town, we can walk and pray. I find that walking keeps my body active (it is difficult to fidget and walk, for walking is a way of planned fidgeting). Walking frees my mind and spirit to pray. Especially if anger is fueling my prayer, walking energetically is a good way of expressing it.

We can also use our other senses, such as sight, to add vitality to our praying. If our concern, for example, is for Northern Ireland, we can get a picture that expresses the struggles of that community. A picture of one of the IRA or UVF end-of-terrace murals can put us in touch with the deep fear, hatred, and prejudice that covers the land. Or a picture of a parent or family member, who so courageously bore witness to his faith by forgiving those who killed a child, can aid our praying for the raising up of a generation of Christians who will endeavor, despite the cost, to overcome evil with good. (See further on this in the section on making a prayer journal, in the Postscript.)

The rosary is a means of prayer that is connected to the sense of touch. Neville Ward's book, *Five for Sorrow, Ten for Joy,* is a fine Methodist meditation and instruction on its use. It is worth remembering that Wesley's rosary is one of the "holy relics" still kept today. Those of us with a Protestant background may shy away from such an aid to prayer. We may have to get in touch with prejudice to break free. Equally we may need to find other "touching" aids to prayer.

I have a tree stump from a peat bog in Scotland in my prayer "line of sight." Although I do not touch it much, I often look at it and reflect on the beauty of that piece of wood shaped under great pressure for two hundred years. It is an aid to praying for creation and for society for it was laid down through the Clearances—that horrific act of vandalism toward creation and injustice toward the needy, which so scarred the countryside and the community in Scotland in times past. It inspires me to pray against similar injustices today, as well as to have confidence that God cares for the abused and can sculpt beauty even out of injustice. In these and other ways, we are to stretch our praying skills and use our whole being in prayer.

With this preliminary, we turn now to the prayers of Scripture. In doing so I want to draw attention to four great themes of those prayers. As you explore and practice these themes, other ones may well come to you. In that case, integrate them into your prayer for the world.

Hope

I could equally well have used the words *despair* or *lament,* for what seems to give energy and urgency to so many of the prayers of Scripture is the gulf between what is and what could or ought to be. It is this gap that provokes and kindles prayer. Just as an electric current will jump between two points, creating a spark that can ignite a fire, a cooker, or an engine, so prayer can spark off a major work of God when it sees the gap between what is and what should be, which is why lament, grief, and wailing play such a part in biblical prayers.

Hannah weeps before the Lord for a child, and is neither put off by Eli accusing her of being drunk, nor by her husband saying, "Don't I mean more to you than ten sons?"

(1 Sam. 1:8). Hannah's state is as clear an answer as he could wish to have, if only he could see it! Hezekiah's prayer for healing, and Bartimaeus' prayer for sight, both express the same agonized struggle to discover from God what seems a million miles from where they are.

At a national level, Nehemiah (Nehemiah 1) grieves over Jerusalem, not just because of the bad state it is in, but because it is so far from God's purpose for his city. Moses on the mountain cries out for Israel because they are so wayward, so far from God's plan for them. Daniel's prayer for Jerusalem (Dan. 9:4–19, especially 17–19), or Paul's prayer for Israel (Rom. 9–11, and especially 9:1–4, and 10:1) follow this same "gulf dynamic" of grief and hope.[3]

So I could have headed this section "grief" or "lament," but I have entitled it "hope" (the other end of the spectrum) because we live in a society so lacking in hope. It may be easier for us to be in touch with what is wrong than with what the coming of the kingdom might look like. This is so because in the West, the twentieth century, which began with high (humanistic) hopes of progress, ended on a note of hopelessness. Apart from a hope that things may get better materially, there is little or no other hope. As Mother Teresa so rightly said, in the West there is "a famine of hope." Much of the urban violence and pointless vandalism is an outworking at the social level of hopelessness, as is the use of drugs. So, for example, one of my prayers was simply a response to a throwaway line in a TV news item, that there are 10,000 drug addicts in Glasgow. My response was to pray for hope, meaning, purpose, value, and self-worth to be poured out on that drug community—through the church in that fine city.

Christian prayer should focus on hope, and draw on the riches of Scripture to that end. Not that hope should be used as a sticking plaster to remove the ugly sight of despair, but as the salve to wash people's wounds.

The kingdom is the primary picture when it comes to praying with hope: "Your kingdom come" is the fundamental Christian prayer. Our prayers will be greatly enriched if we take hold of the promises of God and pray that they may come to fulfillment in the life of the world and be embodied in the life of the church. We can use Ephesians 5:22–32 to pray for marriages, and for the church as the Bride of Christ. Ephesians 3:14–21 is a wonderful prayer to "pray back" (in the manner outlined in Chapter Seven) on behalf of individuals or church communities, not least those going through times of testing or upheaval, that they may embody what Pope Paul VI called a civilization of love.

Some of the servant songs of Isaiah can give life to our prayers for the life of the nation and the world community. I have found the flow of Isaiah 11 another helpful pattern to rest on in my praying for communities and nations. The flow is from weakness (11:1), through likeness (11:2–3) to justice (11:3–5) and on into peace for the whole created order (11:6–9) and God's purposes through his people (11:10–16). It formed a fruitful basis of prayer among a group of church leaders recently. This passage enlarged our vision, and so strengthened and guided our praying. We are to harness our prayers to the hope that is revealed in Scripture.

Character

If we could stand back from our prayers for others, just for a moment, we would see how easily we pray for improved circumstances but how difficult we find it to pray for enlarged character. Yet the emphasis in Scripture is much more on character than circumstances.

When we pray for healing, when we share our prayer needs, and when we pray for one another in difficulties, we focus on praying for life to be easier. Now, I do not want to discourage prayer for healing, or loving concern for people going through difficult times such as marriage breakdown, bereavement, or redundancy. What I must do, however, because the Scriptures tell us so, is to point out that most prayers in Scripture are about people remaining faithful under pressure rather than about the end of the pressure.

Typical of such an approach are Paul's prayer requests from prison. Over half a dozen times he asks for prayer. Once he asks that he may get out, but all the rest are prayers that he may "boldly declare the gospel" where he is.

The same emphasis on prayer for character above circumstances is evident in the first recorded prayer meeting of the early church. Peter and John had just been released from prison, with strict instructions "not to speak or teach at all in the name of Jesus" (Acts 4:18). They come home to the believing community who lift up their voice and spread before God the dire straits that they are in, ending with the plea "Now Lord, consider their threats" (Acts 4:29). Can you imagine how a Western church might complete that sentence? If we are honest we would have to admit it would be about putting an end to this opposition, or about protecting us from further trouble. But that is not the prayer of the early church. Theirs is a prayer for courage to defy orders, the strength to stay true under duress. So the prayer is:

> Now, Lord, consider their threats and . . . enable your servants to speak your word with great boldness.
>
> —Acts 4:29

We normally pray for the circumstances to change, rather than for the testing and purifying of the character of the person involved. Frankly, it is embarrassing to do so. And we had better be careful in moving into this sort of praying. We are so unused to it that we may all too easily lapse into judgmental prayers. It is as important to proceed with caution, as it is to proceed.

If we are to pray in this biblical way, we need some understanding of why adverse circumstances befall believers. There seem to be two particular reasons. First, there is a work of refining and purifying going on. Peter says:

> Now for a little while you may have had to suffer grief in all kinds of trials. These have come so that your faith—of greater worth than gold, which perishes even though refined by fire—may be proved genuine and may result in praise, glory and honor when Jesus Christ is revealed.
>
> —1 Peter 1:6–7

It is important to remember the difference between testing in an exam, which is to find out whether you have passed or failed, and the testing by fire of a metal. The latter testing is always positive. It will burn out the "failure" and leave the metal (and, by analogy, the person) a richer, finer, more valuable item at the end.

The other reason for difficult experiences in life is that they are part of our calling to enter into the mission of Christ. It is the result of being holy in a fallen world. We are called to overcome evil with good, and that will take us by way of the Cross. This is why, although it may be natural to pray for a change of circumstances ("May this cup be taken from me," Matt. 26:39), God may well have some deeper purpose in taking us by another way ("Yet not as I will, but as you will," Matt. 26:39). So, for example, it may only be by staying true in the face of false accusations in the work situation that evil motivation in the person in authority will be creatively confronted. It may seem more "Christian" to give in, or look the other way, but often confrontation is our calling. Our prayer must be that those so called will be given grace and boldness to overcome evil with good (Rom. 12:21). On several occasions I have watched Christians standing up where no one else had the courage to do so. They did it out of a sense of call, as well as a sense of the injustice of the situation. Because they had the support of a loving and praying community, and because they dared (as children of the Father who cares) to risk reputation, employment, and prospects in the name of justice, they were able to overcome evil. Our prayer for them is a vital part of the spiritual battle.

It is instructive to use Paul's prayers for the churches to which he wrote. They are prayers for character, rather than circumstances. I have found that using them has been a great help. It gives me a starting point, and great riches to ask for. It certainly changes the agenda, which is why we need to let the Scriptures be part of the Spirit's way of lifting us out of an undue focus in prayer on circumstances, into the gospel dimension of character.

Compassion

Some of the most moving prayers in Scripture are inspired and fired by compassion—the longing for the good and welfare of others.

Abraham bargaining with God about how many righteous people there need to be in Sodom and Gomorrah before God will spare those cities is one such prayer. Moses pleading for his name to be blotted out if that will enable God to forgive the children of Israel is another. Paul's prayer in Romans, noted above, is a parallel New Testament prayer. Jesus weeping for Jerusalem is a further example of prayer fueled by compassion—as is the whole book of Lamentations in the Old Testament.

One of the values of using these prayers is that they can often be the means by which God gives us a like compassion in our prayer for others. For instance, to pray for our city using the words of Jesus' prayer for Jerusalem can help us to be in touch with God's compassion for whole communities—as can the use of the relevant parts of the book of Jonah. I frequently use Daniel 9:17–19 in prayer for our nation and civilization.

Furthermore, when we face situations of need and use particular passages of Scripture as the basis for our praying, we know that we are praying in line with the will of God. We are entering into his purposes in the world, and we can have confidence that we are, therefore, praying in line with his will. Without this anchor to our souls, there is always the danger that we will end up simply telling God what to do. As a speaker at General Synod a few years ago graphically put it, "Most people want to serve God—but only in an advisory capacity!" Praying back the Scriptures can deliver us from that approach in prayer.

Blessing

The fourth element of scriptural praying is one of blessing. It was a major feature of the story of the patriarchs in Genesis where charismatic gifting was obviously expected and received as fathers prayed for the next generation. So too we can expect the Spirit to be particularly eager to inspire our praying for the next generation (in family, church, or nation). We can do just that as we use the various blessings of Scripture.

We need not restrict ourselves to the parts of Scripture that deal with prayer as such; rather we can pray back teaching passages as prayers for others. For example, the description of the sevenfold gifts of the Spirit in Isaiah 11:2–3, the fruit of the Spirit as defined in Galatians 5:22–26, or the Beatitudes (Matt. 5:3–10), are wonderful material to give strength and direction to our praying for leaders or others for whom we have a particular responsibility in prayer.

The greatest and most accessible of all such passages, in my experience, is the Aaronic blessing that God told the leaders of Israel to use in putting his name on the people (Num. 6:22–27). Putting God's name on someone means stamping them with the likeness of God, so that they become an icon of God. That is the basis of the meditative exercise that follows. Remember that such praying is not to be restricted to praying for those nearest and dearest to us (although it certainly does include them). Rather, we are commanded not only to wish well for those we love (which is what blessing is), but also to pray for those who misuse us, those who act as if they are enemies of ours, whether they are conscious of that or not. We are to bless those who curse and misuse us. We are to put God's blessing on them. If we are involved in any form of negative relationship, it is particularly healthy to take time to use this meditation as a means of putting God's blessing on those "on the other side" of the conflict. By doing so we are releasing the power of God's kingdom through our prayers.

Finally, it is worth pointing out the Trinitarian structure of this blessing. It is the Father who keeps and protects. It is Jesus who, through his death, has made grace rather than law, the basis of our relationship with God and all creation, and it is the Spirit who brings us peace, shalom, the wholeness of God mediated to us through his presence in our lives.

Prayer Exercise: Putting the Blessing of God on Others

It is best to learn this blessing by heart. It can then be part of the way that we bless others throughout the day (see Chapter Twelve, "Practicing the Presence," for more about blessing). Repeat each phrase several times "over the person,"

- either simply praying wordless prayers of attitude (of blessing)
- or using the praying back method noted earlier of "liturgical sentence" (each line of the blessing) with "charismatic response."

My version is an amalgamation of different translations of this passage.

"The Lord bless you and keep you."

- See the goodness of God streaming out toward the person(s) you are praying for.
- God desires their highest good: be open to some insight as to what that might be.
- Try to name anything you see (such as courage, joy, forgiveness, energy, love, peace, etc.)—the Psalmist spoke often about God as a Refuge.
- See this person "entering God's presence" like a strong tower, finding shelter, comfort, and the strength to go on, to keep faith-filled.

"The Lord make his face shine upon you and be gracious to you."

- See Jesus turning to this person, as he did to the woman in the crowd or to Zacchaeus.
- Rejoice in his compassion; see it filling your attitude toward the person concerned.

Nathaniel, under the tree, being seen and known by Jesus, is another way to see this blessing. Or Jesus turning and looking on Peter with compassion in the moment of his sin.

- See them being, in C. S. Lewis's words, "surprised by joy."

To bless is to "command good": Speak out God's goodness, generosity, help, on this person.

"The Lord lift up the light of his countenance on you and give you peace."

- Recognize that the Holy Spirit knows this person, or group, through and through. There is the smile of God, the waiting of the Father for the prodigal, upon them.
- Name the particular form of God's peace you see is needed to invade the life of this person.

Peace is a rich word that in Hebrew speaks of putting everything back together. It is about proper harmony and balance like a bone reset, a relationship healed, a community celebrating the joy of living.

- Here is heaven breaking in on earth: see it coming down and lifting up the person.
- See glory breaking out: see the person experiencing transfiguration by grace.

Chapter 10

Praying the Lord's Prayer

Do not write it on paper; write it on your heart.

—St. Augustine, on the Lord's Prayer.

A pattern prayer with few words but great themes.

—Michael Ramsey[1]

The Lord's prayer is a summary of the whole gospel.

—Leonardo Boff[2]

The early church did a very thorough job of initiating newcomers into the faith.

That is evidenced both in the New Testament, in which both Gospels and Epistles are instruction books to ground new believers in the faith, and also in the life of the church in the first few centuries. That was expressed in the work of the *catechumenate*—not an easy word to pronounce, or one that we need to repeat often! It refers to the process of preparing candidates for baptism. It was normal for this to take three years. Some schools of Christian initiation included a major work of preparation, particularly during Lent leading up to baptism on Easter Eve. It was done then to underline to the candidates that they were being baptized into Christ's death and resurrection. What better day than the one between those two foundational events of the Christian faith.

The work of nurture of the new believer was taken very seriously for two particular reasons.

The primary one was that people were coming to faith in a hostile culture, where suffering was almost inevitable, imprisonment possible, and martyrdom not out of the question. They had to be prepared well if they were to cope with whatever life, the state, and the devil might throw at them—especially if martyrdom could be on the list of what their "ministry" might be.

The other reason for such thoroughness was that people were being brought into the faith in days before the widespread availability of books. The task of the church was therefore to give people whatever resources they needed to sustain them for the whole journey of faith, in a form that they could remember. Just as today we say to those new to the faith that reading the Bible and praying are fundamental to sustain our faith, so these early Christians were given two particular resources for Christian living. They were called the Presentations, not least, because there was a liturgical "rite of presentation" in which these aids were given to the candidates.

The Presentations were like a map and a compass given to a walker before setting out on a dangerous journey. They remain part of the catechumenate of the church today, in places where that pattern of instruction is consciously continued, as in the Roman Catholic *Rite of Christian Initiation of Adults* (called simply the RCIA). Those two Presentations were, and are, as follows.

The Creed

All too easily we see the Creed as a list of doctrines. It is that, not least as a protection against heresy, but it is much more than that. As John Sanford puts it:

> If you listen to the words of the Creed you will hear, not a statement of doctrine, but a summation of the adventure story of Christ.
>
> —John Sanford[3]

In other words the Creed is what we might today call "a brief history of time" (or "eternity"). It is a distillation of the whole story of God's purposes in the world from its original creation, through his revelation in Christ, on to his ultimate purposes in the redemption of all creation. The Creed also contains a list of resources to sustain us as we participate in God's plan to bring creation to fulfillment in Christ. In this short statement, the new believer was given a summary of the whole story of Scripture. Both the Nicene Creed and the later Apostles' Creed are masterpieces of writing. They are Scripture on the back of an envelope, or, rather, in the heart of every believer.

This meant that when times of testing came, the Christians could remind themselves of God's purposes in the world and of their calling to be part of that work, even if it included much suffering.

What a rich resource this is for the believer. Indeed, I once heard someone say that "the two great commandments were spoken by Jesus in 53 words, the Lord's Prayer in 63 words, the Apostles' Creed in 114 words, the full version of the ten commandments in less than 300 words, but the European Community's regulations on the export of duck eggs runs to 25,000 words!"

The Lord's Prayer

The second of the two great Presentations is the Lord's Prayer. If the Creed reminds us of God's purposes in the whole of creation and the complete course of human history, the Lord's Prayer enables us to find and fulfill our part in that purpose. For to pray "your kingdom come" is to make ourselves available for God and his purpose in our lives. It is a yielding of ourselves to God through prayer. It is also the means by which we draw on God's wisdom, grace, mercy, and strength to fulfill our calling as disciples.

It is, of course, *the* Christian prayer. However, the early Christians had a very different attitude toward it than we do today. Apart from anything else it was greatly reverenced. Candidates for baptism were not allowed to know the content of it until well into year two of their initiation, and then they were not allowed to write it down. It was to be written on the heart. This was not only because of the principle we have already considered ("the word spoken is the word believed"), but because it was considered such a dangerous, and politically subversive, prayer. That may surprise us because it has become a bland prayer to many people today. The early church saw it so differently:

> Allegiance to the empire was determined by proclaiming the kingship of the emperors, the holiness of their name, and submission to their will. To declare otherwise, as demanded by praying the Our Father, was to act subversively towards the powers and principalities.
>
> —Michael Crosby[4]

With these two gifts, the Creed and the Lord's Prayer, the church of the early centuries—a despised, largely uneducated, and persecuted minority—bore faithful witness to Christ, often to the point of martyrdom, and eventually conquered the Roman Empire. We do well to sit at their feet and learn from them how the simple discipline of this prayer can make us witnesses who are as fruitful and faithful to God's grace in our day as they were in theirs.

Overfamiliarity, and abuse in its use, have robbed us of the power and fruitfulness of this prayer. What follows is an attempt to recapture it for the life of the church today. To do that there are four things we need to grasp if we are to engage with its vigor and vitality.

See Its Shape

We are often not best served by well-intentioned preachers who, in seeking to teach the Lord's Prayer, jump straight into an exposition of it line by line. Valuable though this is, it misses the more important fact of the overall shape of the prayer. Grasping the shape is of more importance in learning to pray this prayer, than knowing a great deal about each phrase.

Essentially there is a fourfold pattern.

First is the *address* in which we give attention to God as he has revealed himself in Christ. He is the One who has established intimacy with us as Father, who has made us a community of faith that calls us to address him as "Our" (rather than "My") Father, the One who yet remains, as Isaiah saw him, "high and lifted up," and also the One who inhabits the transcendent glory of heaven. In other words, the prayer begins with our seeing God, with our beholding the throne. This is always the first step in prayer: giving attention to the One to whom we come.

Second, are the *You-prayers,* in which we give attention to God's name being honored, his kingdom coming, and his will being done. These are three different ways of saying the same thing, namely, that what God desires and intends is what matters most to us. Here is the work of conversion being expressed in our prayers, because our attention is first and foremost on discovering God's will and in working on his agenda. We come to God not to say "Your will be changed," but "Your will be done."

Third, come the *Us-prayers,* in which we bring the whole range of our needs to God: material needs ("give us"), relational needs ("forgive us"), and spiritual needs ("conflict deliver us"). Yet even these needs are needs that arise in the course of our seeking to discover and do God's will and be part of his purposes in the world. They are the resources we seek to enable us to go in Christ's name and be involved in the work of his kingdom. They are the needs we have if, in the midst of human sin, conflict, and injustice, we are to live and preach the message of reconciliation. They are the needs of those who have dedicated their lives to overcoming evil with good, and—in the process—discover that they are up against the principalities and powers.

Fourth are the *affirmations* of God's presence with us: "the kingdom, the power and the glory are yours, now and for ever." Prayer ends by a faith-affirmation that God is with us as we "go out into the world," and that Jesus is with us "to the very end of the age" as the final words of Matthew's Gospel put it (Matt. 28:20).

Notice that the encounter framework of *seeing–knowing–going* lies just below the surface of this prayer. The address focuses on *seeing* the One to whom we are coming. The You-prayers and the Us-prayers are the orientation of our lives around the will and grace of God. They express the *knowing* of God, which is the fruit of hungering for his will and his righteousness. The affirmations speak of the strength in which we go in his name; they are the practice of God's presence with us in our *going.*

Once we grasp this overall pattern we can make best use of the prayer. For example, I was recently invited to pray for a sick person—on the basis of "calling for the elders of the church" (James 5:14). We spent the whole evening praying the Lord's Prayer. We took a couple of hours to pray it—although we did have a coffee break in the middle!

We began by giving attention and worship to God as the Father in heaven to whom we could come, with confidence in both his love and his healing power. This time of worship included thanksgiving for God's faithfulness to us in the past and for his presence with us now. We then spent time in intercession for ourselves, and particularly the sick person, that God's kingdom would come, and that we would be able to recognize that coming. Included in this was time spent in listening prayer, being open to what God might want to say and do through our prayers that evening.

We then came to the specific needs of the person who had called us to prayer. In praying for "daily bread" we prayed specifically for physical healing, and included anointing with oil at that point (James 5:14). We also prayed about a broken relationship that had emerged as an issue during our earlier time of listening prayer. Interestingly, James speaks specifically about that in his instructions on prayer for healing (James 5:16). That led on naturally to pray for protection in spiritual attack as a result of the long illness the person had experienced. As we prayed through this aspect we received several "words of knowledge" about barriers to healing that led us into further prayer.

This involved talking with each other, and some crying too—as well as that cup of coffee. A relaxed and affirming atmosphere is very important in such prayer. Without it we can be in danger of taking ourselves, and our part in the work of prayer too seriously. The words of Emperor Hirohito, the last emperor of Japan to be officially recognized as divine, keep my sense of proportion and perspective whenever an atmosphere of false seriousness begins to surface in such a situation. He said:

> "You cannot imagine the extra amount of work I had when I was a god!"

The evening ended on a note of thanksgiving for God's evident presence with us, and affirmation of his presence with us, and specifically with the sick person, in the days ahead. The closing words of Psalm 23 came to mind as we closed, namely:

> Surely goodness and love will follow me
> all the days of my life,
> and I will dwell in the house of the LORD
> forever.
>
> —Psalm 23:6

In summary, once we have grasped this fourfold framework we can use the Lord's Prayer as an invitation to come into God's presence, seek the coming of his kingdom, and go with the confidence that he is with us.

Talk It Back

What has already been said has indicated something of how the Lord's Prayer can best be used—as headings for our own praying. In other words, as we saw in praying back the Scriptures (Chapter Seven), we can use the principle of liturgical sentence and charismatic response to good effect here. Form and freedom are not rivals or alternatives, but fellow-workers in the task of prayer. Tertullian, one of the great teachers of the early church, said of the Lord's Prayer, "Jesus Christ our Lord has marked out for us disciples of the New Covenant a new outline of prayer." That is right, it is just that, an *outline* that invites us to fill in the details.

We can do this not only in our own praying—and often my prayer time is simply taking fifteen to twenty minutes to pray this prayer—but also in praying with others. The story of the healing prayer above is one such way. In another, very different, and difficult, conflict situation, I was also able to bring the group involved together by praying our way through this fourfold framework as we addressed the issues that divided us. Through praying it together his kingdom was coming.

Focus It

In all the above illustrations of how I have used this prayer, there is one important point for us to bear in mind, namely, that there is a specific focus to the praying of the Lord's Prayer. This is where the popular use of the prayer is, I believe, so debilitating to its proper use.

I find the use of the phrase *an intentional* helpful at this point. It is the word used by Roman Catholics of a celebration of the Mass for a particular person or situation. So, for example, one might hear that there will be "an intentional Mass for Northern Ireland." It means that there will be a service focused around concern and prayer for the situation in that country.

Equally, in praying the Lord's Prayer I have found it essential to pray it in relation to some well-defined concern. That may be as narrow a focus as my life today, or as wide an issue as the survival of Planet Earth, but both give a focus and direction to the praying. What is important is that we decide what it is that we are praying for. This is part of the prayer of agreement (Matt. 18:19).

This step is simply and easily done, but without it the prayer lacks direction, purpose, and thereby authenticity.

Live It

I have kept the best wine until last, for the greatest secret of the Lord's Prayer is that it was given for a threefold interlocking purpose. First, it was given to teach the disciple how to pray; second, to embody Jesus' whole teaching in a few memorable phrases; and third, to give expression to the way of life that should arise out of such teaching. So, too, the Lord's Prayer is a prayer to be lived as well as prayed. This is why the early church gave it to candidates preparing for baptism as one of the two gospel Presentations. The Creed tells us the story of God's purposes for his world, fulfilled in the person and work of Christ, and awaiting fulfillment at the end of the age. The Lord's Prayer shows us how to join in with God's loving and life-giving purposes.

We are to walk through life living before a holy yet loving Father to whom we continually look up. We are to seek his purpose, will, and kingdom in the whole of our living, trust ourselves to his provision for all we need to live a life of obedience, and celebrate the fact that we are always in his presence.

So our prayer is, finally, a *going*. It is a going that involves living out of obedience to God and in compassion for others. It enables us to break out of any sense of a small area of life being divided off as a spiritual compartment. Rather, in the words of the slogan for one of the chain of gas stations, it becomes "the stop that keeps you going." In this way, praying the Lord's Prayer draws us out of any dull or introverted self-focus into the broad channel of God's mercy and love toward his world. From prayer we rise to go in God's name. So this prayer becomes a pattern for our living, as we love God, work for the coming of his kingdom, trust our needs to him, and dwell always in his presence.

How that final stage, of dwelling in the presence and reality of God, can happen is the subject of the remaining two chapters. But first, a prayer exercise on the use of the Lord's Prayer.

Prayer Exercise: Meditative Aid to Praying the Lord's Prayer

Use this framework a number of times, until you make it your own, then expect your use to grow and change until it is your meditative aid rather than mine. It may well take a month or two of using this outline several times a week to reach that point. "Let us not become weary in doing good, for at the proper time we will reap a harvest if we do not give up" (Gal. 6:9).

This form is a shortened one I use in the normal course of the day. It is easily remembered and enables me to pray the prayer in a short space of time—while waiting at a traffic light or for a meeting to begin, for instance.

Our Father in heaven

- Look up to the God who has made all that is, and rejoice that he knows and cares for you.

He has given us his Spirit, so that we can call him "Abba, Father" (Rom. 8:15; Gal. 4:6).

He is all-powerful, yet he uses his power only in doing good.

- See yourself as part of a worldwide family that is chosen and loved by the Father.
- Rejoice that such a God actively invites us to come before him in prayer.

Your name; Your kingdom; Your will

- God's name expresses his character; meditate on that character and its many-sidedness: creativity, compassion, truth, holiness, justice, peace, mercy.

- Praise God that his "just and gentle rule" has broken into this world, supremely in Christ.
- Praise him for every way in which you are aware of his kingdom coming in your "world."
- Lift to him situations that cry out for the breaking in of his kingdom.
- Listen to the Spirit giving you prayer beyond your understanding for the coming of his kingdom into specific situations.
- Be open to the gift of righteous indignation or compassion as fuel for prayer.
- Let the gulf between what is and what could/should be, generate faith and hope for prayer.
- Expect to be made eager for a new world order in which righteousness and peace dwell.
- Bring your life before God to be available to him in his service.
- Be open to his directions for your living.

Give us; Forgive us; Deliver us

- Be specific in bringing your practical needs to God,

especially those things you need in order to do the will of God. Where you have sinned, own it, give it to God, and receive in its place his forgiveness.

Where you have been wronged, admit it, and release those people from any debt to you.

- Pray for God's blessing on anyone who is your enemy, anyone you find difficult.
- Be open to God showing you any way in which you are involved in a spiritual battle.
- Ask for God's wisdom, strength, protection, and courage to handle that situation.

The kingdom, the power, and the glory are yours . . . Amen

- Affirm the fact that God is with you wherever you are.

- Celebrate the fact that when you leave your time of prayer, God goes with you.
- Look with the eyes of faith, hope, and love on the things that you are about to turn to.

Chapter 11

Discerning the Presence of God

Seeing God in the Whole of Life

Many of us today live in a kind of inner apartheid. We segregate out a small corner of pious activities and then can make no sense of the rest of our lives.

—Richard Foster[1]

The sense of God is vanishing from the earth.

—Pope John Paul II

A culture whose people have lost all sense of their interior lives.

—John F. Kavanaugh[2]

Western society stands today in urgent need of healing. It is a culture that has achieved incredible technological advances, but in the process it has lost touch with its soul, with the spiritual dimension of life, and with ultimate meaning.

The reason for the disease we see around us, and for the sense of moral and spiritual vacuum at the heart of our culture, lies close to the heart of our greatest successes. Our culture is brilliant at analysis. We have analyzed all that is, from ourselves on the psychiatrist's couch, to the atoms that go to make up the couch, the psychiatrist, and the patient. But we have lost a sense of meaning and purpose to life. We have lost touch with our humanity.

> The culture that enthrones things, products, objects as its most cherished realities, is ultimately a culture in flight from the vulnerability of the human person.
>
> —John F. Kavanaugh[3]

The dissected frog stands (or rather lies down!) as a parable of our society. Many of us were required in our school days to dissect these poor creatures, for the cause of the advancement of science, or at any rate, for the passing of exams. In the process we became much more aware of the inner contents of the frog. However, it was quite evident that this was not an advance as far as the frog was concerned. Expert though we have become in understanding its inside, the frog—if it could speak—would be crying out for someone to put it back together again.

That is the cry of our culture today—for someone to show us how to make life work, how to put it back together again, for we seem to have lost so much in the analysis of the parts. As T. S. Eliot put it:

Where is the Life we lost in living?
Where is the wisdom we have lost in knowledge?
Where is the knowledge we have lost in information?
The cycles of Heaven in twenty centuries
Bring us farther from God and nearer to the Dust.

—T. S. Eliot[4]

This is why the great buzz word of the New Age movement is *holistic:* "Making whole" or putting back together again is the desire that is surfacing all around us. Although, as Christians, we disagree with some of the New Age answers, we do well to listen to the cry for wholeness and harmony within ourselves and with all creation.

Discerning before Practicing

This is where the spiritual discipline of practicing the presence of God comes in.

However, as I have reflected on it, I have come to the conclusion that Christians today need to learn a prior discipline, namely, discerning the presence of God. We need to do that because our culture has initiated us into fragmented relatedness; we need to see life as a whole. But also, if we do not first discern God's presence in the whole of life, we will make a fatal mistake. We will imagine that by practicing the presence of God, we are making God present. In a culture built around manufacturing and controlling, that would be all too easy.

But the truth is the opposite. God is already and always present in his world. Our discipline of practicing his presence is simply our tuning in to that Presence. This is what places discerning prior to practicing. Christians in previous ages did not need to learn this discerning, for they lived in a culture with a rich awareness of the supernatural and spiritual dimension.

Prayer of the Heart
Discerning God's presence

As we look for your coming among us,
open our eyes to behold your presence,
strengthen our hands to do your will,
that the world may rejoice and give you praise,
Father, Son and Holy Spirit:
Blessed be God for ever!

—*Celebrating Common Prayer*

This chapter is going to address our currently needed ability to discern the presence of God. Only when that is in place can we safely learn to practice the presence of the all-ready present One. Discerning God's presence is, essentially, learning to see God in the whole of life. It is living in the truth that, "in him we live and move and have our being" (Acts 17:28). I want to highlight a number of areas of life where we can see the presence of God.

Relationships

Unless we are hermits (and therefore probably not near enough to a good Christian bookshop to obtain a copy of this book), people will play a large part in our experience of life. Life being what it is, we are likely to experience either too many, and so feel that our space is being invaded, or too few, and so feel that "nobody loves me." Whatever our relationship with others is, they play a formative part in our experience of life.

Experiencing too many is often a call from God—through the overwhelming demands—to order, or re-order, our private world. God is speaking to us through people, even if only to ensure that our ultimate focus is on him. In such circumstances I have found great comfort, and not a little humor, in a passage from Mark's Gospel. It reads:

> Simon and his companions went to look for him, and when they found him, they exclaimed: "Everyone is looking for you!" Jesus replied, "Let us go somewhere else."
>
> —Mark 1:36–38

Equally, too few, or too difficult, a set of relationships can also be a means of encountering God and hearing him addressing us through the pain and struggles.

However, God gives us good gifts through others too. He speaks to us often through others—Christians and non-Christians alike. Often a seemingly casual aside speaks to our hearts or touches us in some way that is the voice of God to us. Recognize the voice of God, and receive his truth—whoever and wherever it comes from. God also gives us affirmation and a sense of personal worth through others. People say good things to all of us. Sadly we brush it aside. We say, "Oh, it was nothing," when it was actually a difficult thing we did freely for another person. Or we receive a compliment about what we have done or how we look, and dismiss it by turning the conversation onto our struggle beforehand to know how to speak or dress, or whatever it was. Such responses may be natural, but they are neither true, wholesome, nor healthy. They are also a form of put-down to those who have stepped out of their way to pay us a compliment.

But God speaks to us through suffering, brokenness, and pain in others too. This is the thrust of the parable about the sheep and the goats. "When did we see you hungry?" God addresses us in the faces and lives of those who are the weakest. This is why Luther advised pastors to "spend time with things that take life blithely, such as birds and babies." It is good advice: God is not just speaking to us, he is present to us, and blessing us through others in that moment. I think of a couple of Downs syndrome young men in my last church. They greeted people with such warmth and joy and pleasure. I often wondered when I saw them hugging one of our more formal members, and me(!), "Who are the handicapped ones here?"

God also wants us to give something of himself to others whose paths we cross—even if only fleetingly in the check-out lane. Here, I have found that putting the blessing of God on others is a very positive discipline. We can do that without praying any words. Just an *attitude* of blessing is a prayer. Relationships are a primary channel of God's grace in our lives.

Life

"God likes life, he invented it." And it comes to us by grace rather than by works or law. Our very existence is a gift, and all the best things in life start off free. The air we breathe, the soil we till, the seeds we sow, all come from the good hand of a giving God.

This means that to walk in thanksgiving is to be connected to reality. Indeed, I am convinced that if we thanked God more for what we have, such as the pictures on our walls or the clothes in our wardrobes, we would need to spend less time and money buying new ones.

Often God addresses us through life, calling us to yield to his way and priorities in our lives, or provoking us to faith or to action by the very testing nature of what is happening to us. I had been talking to a young wife and mother recently who had been going through some very painful struggles in her marriage, which I had been "strengthening her hand" to act boldly about. After nearly a year of this pain, she said not only that it had been the most difficult and painful year of her life, but that God had spoken to her in and through the pain. Then she added the striking comment; "For the first time in my life, I look inside myself, and I like what I see!" God gives even in the pain. As Neville Ward has put it:

> The process of nature, the flux of history, all that happens to each individual every twenty-four hours is a "sum of things forever speaking."
>
> —Neville Ward[5]

This is what the spiritual writers of old meant by the "blessed sacrament of the present moment." God comes to us in the whole of life. We discern his presence by listening, by hearing, by choosing, by obeying, and by returning thanks for his presence with us.

Creation

Modern life means that most of us are seriously cut off from creation, so much so that what aspects of the created order we do experience we filter out. As someone has said, in the midst of a noisy street in London or New York, most of us "moderns" can hear a coin drop, but we cannot hear the birds singing while we decide whether or not to pick it up.

We need consciously to reconnect with creation (see the poem "Leisure" at the end of Chapter Three). We can do it by *walking in thanksgiving*. We can do it by talking thanksgiving—commenting on the beauty of the sky, or the sound of the bird, or whatever we are aware of.

This connects, too, with our ability to enjoy life, to celebrate our existence and the existence of the whole created order. In our fragmented world we are in grave danger of having a form of spirituality that expresses brokenness, rather than heals it. That happens when we have a narrow definition of what it is to be spiritual. It is not a compartment of life, it is a way of seeing the whole of life. That is why spirituality touches the whole of life; it is the spiritual dimension that restores wholeness, that brings integration to modern culture.

Creativity

We are made in the image of the Creator, and creativity is a whole-making activity. The forms of creativity are endless, and many of us spend most of our time in this aspect of our being. The most obvious form of creativity is work, but it is something much wider than "paid employment." Parents not only have the incredible privilege of bringing a new life into being (surely the greatest expression of creativity), but are also called to create community by "making a family." Creating family is one of the most vital works of our day. Creating pleasing environments, whether by art or clearing rubbish, is another vital task for today's society, as is the task of creating wealth, work, and pleasure.

It is at this point that a super-spiritual, or narrowly spiritualizing, attitude to life misses so much, including the presence of God. All of us, in our places of work, and beyond them, are called—in the image of our Creator—to be creative. It is also an important aspect of discovering who we are, and in the process, discovering and discerning God's presence in the whole of life.

As we saw in the chapter on listening prayer (Chapter Eight), we make vital connection with God as we seek to listen to him about, and in, our work situations. Because of the dualism so widespread in the church today, we are likely to need the help of others at this point, to discern where God is active in our work environment and how we can be faithful to him, not just (or primarily) by evangelizing those we work with, but by evangelizing the whole way the work is carried out. The Hospice movement is one fine example of how Christians have "evangelized" the care of the dying.

It is this, I suspect, that should be occupying much more of the life of the church than it currently does. We often function as Christians as though Scripture said "God so loved the church . . ." when it actually says "God so loved the *world* . . ." (my italics—and his?!). We meet him there, as we listen to his leading, discern the coming of his kingdom, and commit ourselves to overcoming evil with good. Once we gain this perspective we will have much less trouble practicing the presence of God; we will be tripping over it all the time!

We are to pray over the aspects of creativity into which God has called us, in our household or family setting, our local community, our work situation, and our part in the political life of our community and country. Remember, "politics" is about the creative work of "making city."

The Sacred Canopy

We live in a secular culture—although that is rapidly changing. This culture has marginalized any sense of the sacred to the farthest corners of our community's life. It is acceptable to be "religious" in the private realm, but public life—so the assumption goes—deals with real things, real facts, and real dependable principles. The result is that we have lost the sense of the sacred in all of creation, including the moral dimension of life. A recent report from the unlikely prophetic source of the Institute for Economic Affairs has defined the situation well in terms of how personal, and sexual, relationships have been reduced to market forces and a consumer mentality.

> The approved pattern is one of individual entrepreneurs, each free to strike a bargain as producer of sexual gratification with any willing consumer.[6]

That is just one area of the sacred. There are many more. The biblical view is that all of life is sacred. This is the purpose of the ten commandments. They are couched in negative form ("Thou shalt not . . .") to remind us that there are areas of life that are off limits to us. It is a major cause for struggles in medical ethics today that there is really no basis in a modern scientific materialism culture for denying that "if we have the technology, there is nothing to stop us" (such as taking eggs from aborted fetuses). The ten commandments put limits back into life. That is liberating. It means that God can be seen in all the moral issues we face, such as our life focus (idols), use of art (images that are out of bounds), language (taking his name in vain), the need to stop and celebrate (Sabbath), family relationships (honoring parents), property, sexual limits, and the right to life, as well as the one that takes us into the New Testament dynamic of the law in the heart (covetousness, "which is idolatry," Col. 3:5).

We live today with the fact that our abuse of the environment has created a hole in the ozone layer. As a result, life-threatening rays can get in and put everything that exists under threat. It is a parable of what has happened at the moral level. By "liberating ourselves from moral constraint" we have lost the sacred canopy which we need to protect us from the harmful effects of the creature playing God.

The sacred canopy not only sets limits, but it establishes shalom (peace, harmony, balance). It establishes the framework within which connectedness between men and women, humanity and creation, people and property, creatures and Creator can work. As we see moral issues around us, we will find God and his kingdom at work drawing attention to connectedness and balance—the mobile of the cosmos.

Once we see this, we can begin to sense the presence of God, brooding and grieving (Gen. 1:2; Rom. 8:22, 23, 26—the threefold groaning) over the travail of contemporary moral dilemmas and the "valueless" world into which we are educating the next generation. The newspapers and TV and radio news are as good a way of seeking to see the sacred canopy as any. Our world stands in urgent need of re-sacralizing. We assist that missionary endeavor every time we discern the presence of God in the moral dilemmas we face as individuals, families, communities, or society.

Walking in Communion

The sacrament of communion is built around two themes. The first is that of thanksgiving. It is a service of thanksgiving (that is what the Greek work *Eucharist* means) from beginning to end. The prayer exercise that follows is designed to strengthen our ability to walk through the whole of life with an attitude, and in the practice, of thanksgiving. It is the bridge between discerning and practicing the presence of God.

The other theme of communion is what is called the "fourfold action." This refers to the four things that Jesus did when he instituted communion. He took, blessed, broke, and gave the elements to his disciples. The prayer exercise that follows is built around that fourfold action. Henri Nouwen's little book, *Life of the Beloved,* uses this as the basis for "spiritual living in a secular world." As we make ourselves at home in this structure, we will find that we are not only discerning God's presence more readily in the whole of life, but also that we are more immediately at home when we come to receive communion at church.

Prayer Exercise: Practicing Communion

Review the last hour, day, or week.

- Thank God that he is with you now. Then give thanks for the good gifts of life:

- for physical and mental health, which we take so much for granted: receive them now ("hands up") as gifts given new each day.
- for the people in your life without whom you would feel lost or less.
- for the creation around you (for example, within a hundred yards).
- for the areas of creativity in which you are participating: do not focus on the failures; enjoy the gift and opportunity at this point.
- for the moral dimension that is gift to your life.

■ Now picture Jesus coming to you in this setting in your life.

Taking

He knows us, cares about us, takes us in his arms, calls us by name.

In him we belong: We have security, meaning, purpose.

We are not alone in the universe.

We are friends of the Creator.

Surrender to a Love that is affirming and life-giving.

Blessing

You have learned to put the blessing of God on others, now put it on yourself.

Hear God speaking the Aaronic blessing over you. See his eye upon you in affirming love.

Be open, in listening prayer, to particular words of affirmation God may give you now.

Note them, build them into the liturgy of your heart.

Breaking

Trust him with those areas of pain, frustration, and creatureliness with which you struggle at present.

Like the clay, dare to yield to his reshaping.

Remember, it is his re-shaping, not the manipulation or control of others, that we yield to.

Let the process of Cross-and-Resurrection do its enriching work in you.

Giving

See God taking you as a gift that he is giving to those around you.

See him giving you to your family/household, work, community, friends.

Be open to how he desires that gift to be given.

Be aware of any promptings of the Spirit about ways in which he is calling you to give yourself to others.

Conclude by returning to thanksgiving for life, for being part of God's purposes in human history, for God himself.

CHAPTER 12

Practicing the Presence of God

Encountering God in the Whole of Life

In understanding the true nature of prayer, it is a mistake to draw too rigidly the frontier between prayer and life.

—Michael Ramsey[1]

Life is shaped, moment by moment, through an awareness of the "Significant Other" who gives meaning to our reality. Prayer in whatever form is the means to maintaining this awareness.

—Jack Dominian[2]

Now that we have seen how God is present and active in his world, we can start to discover his presence and act on the truth of it, even when we do not have conscious evidence of it. We are ready to tackle the art of "practicing the presence." But what is it?

What it is not, and the previous chapter sought to establish this, is our making God present in a way which, without our efforts, he would not be. We are creatures of the Creator of all that is. So practicing the presence is becoming in touch with what is, not creating what is not.

This practice can be described in a number of ways. One such way is to say that practicing the presence of God is *living out the two great commandments,* to love God and love others as ourselves. It is to live life within the interlocking pattern of love—for God, others, and the self.

Another way of describing practicing the presence is that it is *living in the gospel,* celebrating the good news that God is with us and that he has promised to be with us "to the close of the age." It is discovering the reality of the commandment to "remain in me" (John 15:1–17) and so "bear much fruit."

Equally, it is *living as a child of God* (Luke 18:15–17 with Luke 8:19–21), able to enjoy the present moment, able to look up in wonder and live fully in the present moment, being in touch with ourselves and the surrounding community, and to center our living upon God himself. That includes the capacity to celebrate.

Supremely, it is *the enjoyment of God himself;* as the Westminster Catechism puts it, "our chief end is to glorify God and to enjoy him for ever." However, let me immediately qualify this by saying that this is not some artificial spirituality. Indeed, its heart is the opposite—a capacity to dance, to play, and to be human. It is the capacity not only to enjoy and know the presence of God, it is to receive and enjoy his gifts. A child at Christmas saying "thank you" to its parents for the wrapped present shows appreciation by unwrapping the present and enjoying it. So too for us, the enjoyment of relationship with God includes the ability to enjoy his gifts of creation, humanity, friends, and life itself. As James Philip puts it:

> The deepest word that can be spoken about sanctification is that it is a progress towards humanity. Salvation is, essentially considered, the restoration of humanity to man. This is why the slightly inhuman, not to say unnatural, streak in some forms and expressions of sanctification is so far removed from the true work of grace in the soul.
>
> The greatest saints of God have been characterized, not by haloes and an atmosphere of distant unapproachability, but by their humanity. They have been intensely human and lovable people with a twinkle in their eyes.
>
> —James Philip[3]

To practice the presence of God is to rediscover connectedness, with ourselves, with the whole of life, and with God. An overspiritualizing of it into "conscious awareness of God" is actually to partake of the brokenness of our present culture, which is disconnected and disintegrated. Practicing the presence of God involves both enjoying God as the supreme goal of all that is, and enjoying all that he has given us: it is to celebrate the reality and goodness of the Creator and the creation. Just as you do not do an artist the greatest honor by always looking at him and never at his paintings, so we do not fully enjoy God unless we develop the capacity to enjoy all that is. As C. S. Lewis[4] put it so succinctly, "To experience the tiny theophany (a moment or means of God revealing himself) is to adore." To enter into the playing of a child, the beauty of sun on autumn leaves, or an understanding look from a friend is to be alive to God in his universe.

For this reason, the particular skill that I believe we need to recapture today is this ability to rediscover connectedness or integration, and see all life as in God, and God touching us in the whole of life.

An Important Distinction

Before we move on to consider practical steps that we can take to live before God in the whole of life, I want to underscore an important distinction that Leanne Payne makes in her book, *The Healing Presence.* It is that there is a difference between the practice of the presence and the sense of the presence of God. The *practice* is our part, part of our spiritual discipline; the *sense* of God's presence is his gift to give when and how he chooses. We will not always *sense* God's presence. Indeed, if we did there would be no ground for faith—it would all be by sight. However, as we learn to practice God's presence we will experience moments of great closeness to, and enjoyment of, God. It is right to savor and enjoy such moments, but not make the experience greater than the One experienced. C. S. Lewis's book, *Surprised by Joy,* is the testimony of someone who missed God for many years because he sought the experience of joy rather than the Source of joy.

Into Action

All the previous chapters have ended with a "prayer exercise." This one, because of its subject, needs to be different. What now follows is the "exercise" part of the chapter. As such it contains a whole series of "exercises" that are to be done not in the times we withdraw to prayer, but in the midst of life. It is important not to attempt to become familiar with all of them at the same time. That would be a recipe for spiritual exhaustion. My encouragement, rather, is to take one of them at a time—for a month or two—and develop proficiency in it, making it, as we have seen in other aspects of the prayer life, part of how we pray. It is good to note in one's prayer journal what the focus will be, and any ways in which you sense that progress is being made. If you can work with someone else—a prayer partner, or as part of the life and work of a home group—so much the better.

Do not be discouraged by seeming failures and by "nothing happening." If we exercise the discipline of practicing God's presence, he will give the gift of awareness and awe in his timing and in his ways. And we had better be prepared for God's surprises, his tap on our shoulder to look in the opposite direction from the one we were looking in, for us to see him. This is what Jesus was doing with Peter when he told him to cast the net on the "other side." It was what God was doing with a friend of mine who, when ill, naturally sought prayer for healing from those gifted in that work—only to discover that the healing actually came when he was drinking a pint of beer. God gives himself through the whole of creation. He is the God of surprises. So let's get on with the joyful work of practicing his presence.

Rhythms and Routines

We are creatures of habit, and that is a good thing. But it also suggests how we should handle our praying: by tying it in with the regular patterns of our living. The Celtic Christians were very good at this, and had prayers for lighting fires, prayers for milking cows, and prayers—it seems—for every eventuality.

Few of us light fires, other than by the flick of a switch, and even fewer of us today milk cows! But we do have routines. Walking to work, driving to work, shaving, ironing, cleaning the car, and a thousand-and-one other regular chores that do not occupy the whole of our minds. It is good to make connection between such routines and the discipline of calling on the name of the Lord. Maybe there is a time of the day that you can fix in your mind "I will always pray at . . ."; or maybe there is a detour on your way to work that you can make your "prayer detour."

Where I last worked I walked to my office. It was a five-minute walk, and I decided to commit myself to praying while doing that walk—on some occasions four times a day—there and back. At first I often forgot: To be honest, the norm was to forget, the exception was to pray! However, I stuck at it, and found I was praying more often. Rather than berate myself for not praying, whenever I noticed that I was not doing so, I used it to prompt me to turn to prayer. Within a year I was praying for a part of the walk, even if only the last few paces. Then I discovered a fascinating thing. Initially I had caught myself not praying, and so started to pray. After eighteen months (yes, good habits do take time to grow) I realized that I was sometimes catching myself praying—I had gotten into prayer without being aware of consciously doing so. Be encouraged. Addiction to prayer can become habit forming!

Liturgy of the Heart

I have looked at this in an earlier chapter, but I want to return to it at this point since it is—in my experience—very closely related to the first way of practicing God's presence. Gerard Hughes says:

> Christian tradition recognizes that it is difficult for busy and active people to be still, and that is why many traditional methods of prayer are very repetitive, the repetition being designed to still the mind.
>
> —Gerard Hughes[5]

This is classically true of what is known as the *Jesus prayer,* which runs:

> Lord Jesus Christ, Son of God, have mercy upon me, a sinner.

The art is in learning to write the truth on our hearts so that it becomes part of us. I remember one occasion when I had been speaking. I felt particularly unhappy about both "it" (the talk) and myself. I sat down and called on the name of the Lord, slowly repeating this Jesus prayer. My conscious mind was hardly engaged, but I prayed this prayer perhaps twenty or thirty times. My "attitude" was one of saying it as a cry to God; expressing a sense of failure and despair. Within five minutes I had such a strong sense of the love of God around me that I knew I was "accepted in the Beloved." It did not make any difference to my assessment of the talk, but it certainly made a difference to me, my view of life, and my experience of God.

I have developed, over the years, various "shaving liturgies." At this point I am probably one up on our Celtic forbears because that is possibly one thing they did not have a prayer for! One such prayer has been:

> I am chosen in your grace, accepted in your love, made complete in Christ.

Notice that this is in the form of affirmation of truth, rather than request for anything. We have explored this dimension earlier.

Prayer of the Heart
A Celtic Prayer of Connectedness

Bless to us, O God,
The sun that is above us,
The earth that is beneath us,
The friends who are around us,
Your image deep within us,
The day which is before us.
Amen.

(Note: As a night prayer, replace "moon" for "sun," and "rest" for "day.")

Emotions and the Inner Dialogue

Our emotional life is a vast, untapped resource for prayer and for practicing the presence of God. It has been given to us to energize us for life. Anger motivates us to do something about the situation, tenderness makes us gentle with a suffering person or situation, fear focuses our need to find a way through—or out.

All of our emotions can be "energy for life," simply by "turning the inner dialogue up to God." All of us spend much of our time having a dialogue with ourselves. If we could but hear it, it is often not very complimentary to ourselves—except when insecurity fuels pride and we become "grandiose" and see ourselves as God's answer to everyone's prayer. One ready source of engaging with God is to turn that inner dialogue up to God. It will very often help us to see the situation or issue in a different light. It

Prayer Principle 7

Emotional Energy Is Fuel for Prayer

Many of us do not often feel like praying. But we do feel many other things. We feel sad, angry, relieved, joyful, anxious, puzzled. To pray, all we need to do is harness that emotional energy as fuel that lifts our prayers, and ourselves, to God.

will open us up to new and more creative solutions than our instinct to "shoot them all"!

Turning the inner dialogue up to God involves sharing with him our actual thoughts and feelings, listening to the underlying attitudes to ourselves and others (whether of pride, or its cousin, self-pity), and listening to God's answer to what is going on within. Much of the Psalms is the account of the Psalmist's inner dialogue coming out—and going up to God. It is a vital way of staying connected to God.

Listening in Life

Francis MacNutt, in his book *Healing,* says that we should learn to listen to people with one ear, while turning the other one to listen to God for his will and word in the situation. That is how we are to live in the whole of life—listening to God. As we do so, we walk in, and into, his presence. By contrast, Paul Tournier says:

> Listen to all the conversations of the world, those between couples and those between nations, and you will find that they are for the most part dialogues of the deaf.

The Christian is called to listen. We saw this in the chapter on listening prayer, but it is more than an agenda for prayer, it is a way of life. It involves listening to others, to body language, to the hidden agenda, to the strong emotions that often run just below the surface of many a clinically detached conversation.

It also involves listening to our own emotions, as Jesus did in Gethsemane. The first thing he did was to tell the Father how he felt. Only then could he discover God's will. Listening to our own emotions connects us with ourselves. Connection with God comes more easily after that.

We listen to God's call when it comes to us through the challenge of circumstances we are placed in. Prayer can be a thought, an attitude, rather than a verbal action. In that thought we recognize the sacredness of all life, and seek to make a response that pleases God.

In, and beyond, all these ways, we are to listen to God; for to be a Christian is to live out of response to the call of God in the whole of our living. Just as Jesus "only did what he saw the Father doing" (John 5:19), so we are to stay in tune with God. Paul's advice to the Colossians was to "let the peace of Christ rule in your hearts" (Col. 3:15); "ruling" means "acting as arbitrator." We are, as the Quakers say, to "follow our peace." I have found, on a number of occasions, where I have had to make decisions with limited information (a permanent human state, as I now see it), I have sought to decide by choosing what I can best live with if I am proved wrong by subsequent events.

Many Other Ways

Most, if not all, of what has been said in this book can be practiced, not only in specific times of prayer, but as attitudes to life and ways of practicing the presence of God. So, for example, what we have just been considering is simply the moment-by-moment practice of the *listening prayer* that we looked at in Chapter Eight.

Beholding the throne can be done in a moment by carrying in our hearts the words "Our Father." It is not necessary to say them, just to see them; or rather, like icons, to see through them to the truth and reality and glory of God to which they make a way open. Equally, the exercises taught so far, all have "practicing the presence" applications.

Waiting for a bus at the end of an afternoon shopping, or after a busy day at the office, is a natural time to practice the *"letting go before God"* exercise. You do not need to sit down to do it, but it helps to let your hands hang down so you can sense your trials and strains pouring out of your fingers. Hands turned forwards can be expressive of waiting to receive gifts of life. This is also a good time to put the *blessing of God* on people; joy to the glum, friends for the lonely, peace for the restless, faith for the self-confident, can all be "put" on those around us.

Being of a mischievous and economical nature, I have found a way—since becoming an occasional commuter on the London Underground—of reading other people's newspapers with a good conscience. I simply look for headlines which I can turn into *prayers of lament,* or *prayers of blessing.* It makes a game of prayer, but then salvation is, in part, restoration of our ability, and permission, to play in the universe—before the Father.

Summary

I began, way back in the introduction, by explaining why someone, called to help the church evangelize, should get "distracted" into writing a book on prayer. It is appropriate therefore, as I bring this section, on *going* as a result of meeting God in prayer, to a close, to make the connection between prayer and evangelism.

The mystics of medieval times said that evangelism is the sharing of the fruits of contemplation. And so it is. The only authentic good news we have is the good news of our present encounter with God. The more widely that stream flows, overflowing the narrow channels of intercession, fellowship, and public acts of worship, to irrigate the whole of life, the more complete and integrated we will be, and the more will be multiplied the points of connection with a world that is hungry for contact with Ultimate Reality. Which is why, making contact with the whole of life, and being in touch with ourselves, others, life, creation, and God are such evangelistic endeavors. If we could but live that way we would find many asking us for "a reason for the hope that is in us" (1 Peter 3:15), for the knowledge of God does bring hope, and that is a scarce commodity in today's culture.

I ended the introduction with the story of Abba Joseph speaking about being "all flame." So now I end on the same note, by recounting the comment made of St. Francis, which surely expresses the desire of our hearts, for . . .

> It was said of St Francis that he "seemed not so much a man praying as prayer itself made man."
>
> —Richard Foster[6]

God grant that we may enter into such fullness of life, as God has made possible for all, in Christ. May the glory be all his, as the blessing will assuredly be all ours, and those whose lives are touched by God's life in us, as we discover prayer as a deep and joyful affair of the heart.

Postscript

Implementation, Practicalities

Training in prayer should be the main preoccupation and service given by bishops and clergy to the adult members of the church.

—Gerard Hughes[1]

Too little prayer is an expression of unbelief in God's love and care; so is too much.

—Richard Lovelace[2]

There are several things I want to say by way of conclusion concerning the practice of prayer. I have two things to say to individuals: one is a health warning about too much prayer, and the other is about making and using a prayer journal. Then I want to make some suggestions about how the material in this book can help in corporate prayer, and how corporate prayer can strengthen personal prayer. This dimension of fellowship in prayer covers the application of this material in home groups and whole churches.

Too Much Prayer Can Damage Your Spiritual Health!

It may seem a strange way to end a book on prayer, by warning of the dangers of too much prayer, but it is necessary. And it is not just too much prayer that is the danger. The harm comes from taking ourselves too seriously, and by acting out of (often unconscious) pride, which imagines that prayer is simply "something I do." Prayer is a partnership. It should not take us long to work out who is the senior partner.

Our problem stems from living in a self-centered, technological society addicted to taking control. When archaeologists come to dig up the remains of twenty-first-century Western civilization in a few thousand years' time, they need to dig up a remote control unit—it is the primary artifact of our culture. Control without effort, without contact. Take that mentality into prayer, and we will be in for trouble, for to assume that our prayer life is primarily dependent on us is what will seriously damage our knowledge of God.

We had better remember that we can sin by the way we pray (remember the parable of the Pharisee and the publican). The sin I have in mind is that of thinking that prayer all depends on us and our effort. Remember, sin has been defined as our determination to manage by ourselves. All prayer that stems from trying too hard, taking ourselves too seriously, and any drivenness is unhealthy prayer.

From beginning to end we are sustained by God and his grace. We may be able to exist without other people, but we can no more exist without God than a television picture can exist without electricity. It is God who is the primary agent in sustaining our prayer life, which is why opening up to God is a vital first step in prayer. He is the One who draws our heart after him. He is the One who keeps us growing in prayer.

God as Initiator of Our Praying

We do well to remember the other side of the whole thrust of this book. Looking back we can see all the truths about prayer that we have explored, *from God's side.* It is the greater truth.

- *God has encountered us.* Our encounter is a response to his initiative. "Discipleship is first and foremost a response to an invitation" (Henri Nouwen in his foreword to *We Drink From our Own Wells,* by Gustav Gutierrez).
- *God beholds us.* He never forgets us (Isa. 49:15). He will never leave or forsake us (Josh. 1:5; Heb. 13:5). Our names are written on the palms of his hands (Isa. 49:16).
- *God's Word takes hold of us.* We came to faith because God spoke his life-giving Word into our lives. We continue because he continues to do so. His Word "will not return to me empty, but will accomplish what I desire and achieve the purpose for which I sent it" (Isa. 55:11). Whether God's Word comes to us as a hammer (Jer. 23:29) or honey (Ps. 19:10), it is the power of God and will do its work in us.
- *God is always listening to us.* His ear is attentive to the cry of his people, he knows their suffering and he comes down to deliver them (Exod. 3:7–8).
- *God intercedes through us.* It is the Spirit who prays through us. It is God who prays in and through us. He

gives us the gift of intercession. We do not have to work it up. It is the Spirit who enables us to cry, "*Abba,* Father" (Rom. 8:15), the Spirit who alone enables us to say, "Jesus is Lord" (1 Cor. 12:3), and the Spirit who breathes life, energy, and often the very words themselves, into our formless, or half-formed, prayers (Rom. 8:26–27).

- *He practices his presence in us.* He took the initiative in the incarnation to be Emmanuel—God-with-us. He gave us the Holy Spirit to be with us always:

  - Every day is Christmas Day—Christ born in us.
  - Every day is Easter Day—Christ risen among us.
  - Every day is Pentecost—the Spirit poured out upon us.

All we need are buckets of faith big enough to contain such generous outpourings.

We do well to remember these things when we have any wrong sense of achieving in prayer. We also need to hold on to these things when we are too ill or weak to pray. Another is with us. Another is in us. It is all done by grace. As Richard Lovelace puts it when he eschews the use of "spiritual ladders" as a way of instruction in prayer:

> Ladders are always intimidating, and it is my suspicion that Christians should always assume that they start each day at the top of the ladder in contact with God and renew this assumption whenever they appear to have slipped a rung.
>
> —Richard Lovelace[3]

Whenever we take ourselves too seriously, or become over-anxious about our effort in prayer, we would be well advised to meditate our way through the italicized list of this section, and recover perspective—for the glory of God, and the good of our own souls.

Creating a Prayer Journal

Throughout this book, I have attempted to be practical and to avoid writing another book that simply leaves people better informed about prayer. My desire has been to leave the reader better formed in prayer. For this reason I want to add some comments about the practical details of how to develop both personal prayer and corporate prayer through the use of this book.

As far as the aspect of personal prayer is concerned, the whole book has been geared to that goal. There are plenty of exercises to keep an active pray-er going for years. My encouragement is to use the book in this way. Having read this far, the best way to use it is to keep it near wherever you usually pray, and to dip into it, developing one aspect of your *seeing, knowing,* and *going* as appropriate. Keep at it long enough, through that discipline of what C. S. Lewis called "counting the steps," until you have made it your own and it has become part of how you pray.

However, there is one aspect of personal prayer that I have hinted at, but not pulled together in a coordinated way so far, and I want to add a few practical suggestions about it. It concerns the matter of creating and using a prayer journal.

My "prayer journal" is scattered around the room in which I normally pray, with icons on the walls, a pottery chalice and patten on the sideboard, a tape recorder, and my journal in a spiral "reporters notebook" on the table beside the chair in which I sit. I say this to reassure less than totally organized people that you can pray even if you are like that!

However, it could be better organized. It would be if I did not have the luxury of my own study. Here is how I would set about such an organization.

I would use a small ring binder with three major dividers in it. Yes, you have guessed, the divisions would be seeing, knowing, and going.

Seeing

In the *seeing section* I would paste in icons that spoke to me, as well as other pictures, and the words of hymns that found an echo in my experience and approach to God. My own or other people's prayers of adoration would find a home here, as would anything else that aided me in my seeing of God.

Knowing

The *knowing section* would almost certainly be the longest one. This is the value of a looseleaf approach—you can make each section just as long or short as is appropriate. In this part of the journal I would have a number of different elements. Ideally they might be subdivided from each other; in reality they get jumbled up in my journal simply according to the date on which they came to me. I actually find that filing by date is one of the best ways, as I can easily forget which heading I put something under, but I usually have a fair instinct for when I thought or wrote that particular entry. All too easily, for me, filing systems lapse into "a convenient way of losing things alphabetically"!

Nevertheless, here are the various elements in my prayer journal. First are prayers. Among these are set prayers that

I use regularly. For example, one of my favorites is the collect from the Alternative Services Book (1980), which I use in connection with renewing my awareness of being called by Love (see p. 88).

I also write down *some* of my own prayers in my journal. Which ones? Well, the ones that I sense resonate with my life, are God-given prayers, and need to be prayed repeatedly until they are part of the liturgy of my heart. They will often take the form of an affirmation, rather than a request. One such prayer I have used recently, is:

> The God of the universe celebrates my existence.
> Alleluia.

So any prayer that I sense should become part of me, I write down—usually with an asterisk beside it. I do the latter because I also write other prayers which are dealing with an important matter *today,* but which I do not think will be part of a continuing prayer. Leanne Payne quotes a person who said, "How can I know what I think until I hear what I say," which I find very true for my prayer life. Writing it down is important in the process of getting it out. Which is also why I pray out loud—although not loudly!

In this section on *knowing* I also record what I sense God has been saying to me. This may take the form of verses from Scripture, or some way in which my praying back the Scriptures has touched me deeply. Here also I record the words that have come to me as I have sought to practice listening prayer. I write down all that comes, and then, reviewing it later, I put an asterisk on any that seem to be of abiding importance.

I also record dreams that are saying something important, and the reflections on them that emerge from praying them back to God.

Going

The final part of a prayer journal is the *going section.* Here I would have a page for my intercessions list(s), although I kept this simple because I have spent too much of my Christian life laying unreasonable burdens for prayer on myself. I found great liberation through the comment of Richard Lovelace quoted on page 138.

This section would also include pictures that speak to me of our mission in prayer and in life—a picture of pollution to aid my intercession for the care of the environment, and a picture from Bosnia, Somalia, or Northern Ireland to aid the focus of my prayer for those troubled environments.

It is good to keep a page with a list of major events coming up in the next few months, over which I could be praying.

This is also where I would put those prayers that assist my practicing the presence of God, including, for example, the one from *Celebrating Common Prayer,* on p. 167.

Lest this all sounds too holy and disciplined to be true, let me add that I do not pick up my prayer journal every day (even every week). There are seasons where I use it daily, and seasons when it has time off for a few weeks. It is an aid, not a duty.

Implementing in a Prayer or Home Group

Ever since Jesus taught his disciples to pray "Our Father . . ." Christians have discovered how much stronger their prayer life can be if it is a corporate experience. That is not to suggest that corporate prayer is a substitute for private prayer. However, I do believe that corporate prayer is the foundation for private prayer. It roots us in a community, gives us some corporate disciplines, and enriches our prayer through exposure to the prayers of others.

I commend, therefore, the idea of using this book as a basis for corporate prayer in a home group. It would simply be a matter of the group agreeing to do so. Each person would need a copy of the book, and different sections of the material could be worked on from time to time. Maybe once or twice a month, half an hour could be spent doing one of the exercises.

On another occasion an evening could be spent talking over, and then practicing, a whole chapter. It would be best if everyone read the chapter—ideally a week or more in advance of the meeting—and then sought to practice the particular content. At the meeting, after a brief summary of the chapter by someone, people could share joys and sorrows, seeming successes and failures with each other. Remember, sharing sorrows, struggles, and frustrations is as great a blessing as sharing glorious successes, for it keeps the conversation real, rather than ideal, and draws out of others insights and care for the person who has opened her or his heart.

It would be important for the evening to end with the practice of the material, in the light of the group's reflections and experiences. In this way the personal discipline of prayer would be greatly strengthened and affirmed, and the book might become the group's "prayer book" for a few years. There might be seasons when several weeks are devoted to working on this material, and other times when a half-hour practice once or twice a month was sufficient, to sustain mutual support and growth in prayer.

Implementing in the Church

My final word is to church leaders and clergy who have the opportunity to help the whole church bring about the renewal of personal prayer. We may preach often enough on prayer, but this rarely results, in my experience, in a significant movement or increase in its practice.

Our problem is that we handle the preaching ministry in isolation from the total training environment of the church. It simply does not work if treated like that. We need to see that there is a preaching–teaching–training–talking continuum at work in the church. By this I mean that when we discern that God is wanting something to be "birthed" in the church, then the whole life of the church needs to be geared to that end.

So, for example, to stand a chance of renewing personal prayer in the life of a church one would be best advised to take a whole series of steps. Here is a possible program. There is nothing fixed about it. Each local church should adapt the ideas. The important point is that every area of the life of the church needs to be incorporated if the church is to be an effective teaching environment. Your situation may call for a very different approach in one or more of these elements. That is fine. The vital thing is that some connection with the renewal of personal prayer should be made across the board. It is this lack of the wholeness, and so wholesomeness, of the teaching environment that causes isolated sermon series to be seemingly impotent to bring about change. The horse is not connected to the carriage. The engine of truth is not in gear with the wheels of change.

Here then is a suggested strategy for renewing personal prayer in the life of a whole church.

It would be good to gain as wide *agreement* as possible that this was the right aim, and the necessary priority—maybe over the period of a whole year. Indeed, a church council that agreed to such an emphasis could usefully set up a small *monitoring group* that could find out the extent of people's prayer life by use of a sensitive (maybe anonymous) questionnaire at the beginning of this exercise, and then repeat the questionnaire a year later. Monitoring can also be done at a more anecdotal level by asking people how they are getting on with all this prayer stuff the pastor is going on about!

Such a plan does not mean that nothing else would be taught or done—that could result in overkill—but rather that this would be the underlying theme, and one to which, after each Festival, the church returned.

It might well be good to start with a pump-priming *teaching weekend* in which the *seeing–knowing–going* framework was outlined and—as far as possible—practiced.

Preaching could valuably pick up and illustrate the theme of prayer, for example, by a series of sermons on encounters with God, or the Lord's Prayer, or the prayers of Scripture, or through exposition of some devotional psalms. In this way the attention of the church can be brought back to the theme regularly.

Home groups could be encouraged to use the material as outlined in the previous section.

Obviously the aim is that *individuals* practice this material. To aid this, in addition to what is already suggested, it would be good for individuals who have experienced God through a renewed prayer life to be invited to share the same with the whole congregation. It would also be valuable for the subject to be on the agenda of *personal conversations* as part of pastoral care. Paul clearly practiced this type of ministry. He says to the Ephesian church leaders, at the end of his ministry with them, "You know that I have not hesitated to preach anything that would be helpful to you but have taught you publicly and from house to house" (Acts 20:20).

However, when all the above has been done, there is one missing ingredient, which is of tremendous importance. It is all part of implementing in the local church, and is of sufficient importance to deserve a section of its own.

Implementing in Public Worship

The church's coming together involves a whole number of symbolic actions (whether it is officially a "liturgical church" or not) that give identity, meaning, and significance to the whole group and to the individuals in it. That is why people come, to belong to a group with this particular set of interests, concerns, and values in common. Public worship therefore provides a vital time for teaching and training by the whole way it is conducted.

If our goal is to renew personal prayer, then the more that what we are encouraging individuals to do on their own is supported and reinforced when we come together (in home groups, committee meetings, and teams) but especially in the corporate acts of community making which is what Sunday worship is, the greater will be the effect.

So how do we set about communicating about personal prayer through public acts of worship, apart from preaching? Basically by building it into every aspect of the worship. So, for example, the *opening part of the worship* could be consciously related to our seeing of God. It might be appropriate to have a verse from a hymn on the duplicated notices, or on the overhead projector, and invite people to focus on God in preparation for the service. Many churches today are a hubbub of noise before the service. One can either stand up and ask people to be quiet and give them a focus to their *seeing* a minute or two before the service, or do it as the first five minutes of the worship (after giving a welcome and any notices).

The *confession* should tie in with the material on "Good Grief" and should carefully model how to make confession.

Readings from Scripture can be followed by sixty to ninety seconds of silence between the end of the reading and the use of the response "This is the Word of the Lord: thanks be to God." If you are going to do this, people need to be prepared for it—not least if they are used to following the passage in the church Bibles, since they will all shut their books when they are supposed to be meditating on the text!

The *intercessions* are obviously of vital importance in modeling the "how" of personal prayer. Material from the relevant chapter could be picked up and used in leading the intercessions. A useful monitoring job is for someone to record the amount of time actually allocated to silence. The practice is so widespread of those leading in prayer saying "Let us in silence pray for . . ." and then leaving no time for silence—or often, in my experience, just about enough for me to register that I can dare to let go and pray myself, but not enough time to do so!

Again, the *Lord's Prayer* is something that should play a vital part in personal and corporate prayer. If, as the material on the subject in this book argues, we think that the Lord's Prayer needs to be focused, then it is vital that those leading in worship do actually do so before leading the church into the use of it. Using a sung form can also enhance its value, as can the use of it as headings for a whole section of intercession. When we do that we are modeling prayer for each individual.

This is not a complete list of implementing the renewal of personal prayer in public worship, but I hope it is sufficient to enable those who conduct public worship to see how crucial what we do together on Sunday is to the shaping and strengthening of what we do in private during the week. Equally it can seriously undermine it if the connection is not properly made. My conviction, born of experience, is that training in prayer (or any other matter) is not to be measured in terms of:

> personal prayer + home group prayer + preaching + practice in Sunday services = transformation

but rather by the equation:

> personal prayer x home group prayer x preaching x practice in Sunday services = transformation

In other words, each element multiplies, rather than just adds to the effect of the other elements and the fruitfulness of the whole process. However, the mathematically alert will have already spotted that if any item is zero then the whole result is zero. So each element needs to be in place.

If we could but get our act together, in allowing the work of renewing personal prayer to shape the renewal of corporate prayer, and, at the same time, allow the practice of corporate prayer to reinforce the renewal of private prayer, we might see something very significant happening in the life of the church today. It is my conviction that the only authentic good news we have to proclaim is that which has touched our heart in the intimacy of prayer. I repeat the quote from John Talbot:

> We cannot give what we do not have, we cannot evangelize others until God has evangelized us.
>
> —John Michael Talbot[4]

The prayer exercise that awaits us is the total work of personal prayer and, in so far as we have responsibility for it, the renewal of the prayer life of the home group or local church. We can know that any steps in that work delight the heart of the God who delights in us. Such work is life-giving participation in God's purposes for his whole creation. May we find joy in knowing that we are part of that great work.

Notes

Introduction

1. p. 100.
2. *Blessings: Reflections on the Beatitudes,* p. 18.
3. *Prayer: Letters to Malcolm,* Fount, p. 12.
4. Ibid., p. 6.

Chapter 1

1. *Dynamics of Spiritual Life,* Paternoster Press, '79 p. 88.
2. The Preface, opening sentence.
3. Quoted by Leonard Foley in *Slowing Down the Our Father,* St. Anthony's Press, USA, '86 p. 7.

Chapter 2

1. *Our Knowledge of God,* p. 3.
2. *Cycles of Affirmation,* Darton, Longman, and Todd, London, '75 p. 121.

Chapter 3

1. Quoted by Leanne Payne in *The Healing Presence,* Kingsway Publications, Eastbourne, '89 p. 161.

Chapter 4

1. *The Cry of the Deer,* Triangle/SPCK, London, '87 p. 15.
2. *The Earth is the Lord's,* Farrar, Straus, & Giroux, New York, '78.
3. *The Forgotten Father,* Hodder & Stoughton, London, '80 p. 180.
4. *Blessings,* St. Paul Publications, UK, '91 p. 97.

Chapter 5

1. *To Pray and to Love,* p. 77.
2. *Life of the Beloved,* Hodder & Stoughton, '92 p. 43.
3. *Encounter with God,* T&T Clark, '83 p. 5.

4. *The Meaning of Persons,* p. 228.
5. *The Healing Presence,* Kingsway Publications, '89 p. 48.

Chapter 6

1. *To Pray and to Love,* p. 12.
2. *Healing the Shame that Binds You,* p. vii.
3. *The Healing Presence,* Kingsway Publications, Eastbourne, '89 p. 48.
4. Quoted from John Bradshaw, *Healing the Shame that Binds You,* Health Communications, Florida, '88 p. 125.
5. *Sharing Possessions,* SCM Press, London, '81 p. 49.
6. *The Shining Levels,* Fontana, p. 45.

Chapter 7

1. *God of Surprises,* Darton, Longman, & Todd, '85 p. 46.
2. *The Broken Image,* Kingsway Publications, '81 p. 146.

Chapter 8

1. *The Divine Imperative,* p. 66.
2. *Prayer,* Hodder & Stoughton, London, '92 p. xi.
3. *Five for Sorrow, Ten for Joy,* Darton, Longman, & Todd, '93 p. 3.
4. *The Broken Image,* Kingsway, '81 pp. 151–52.
5. *God of Surprises,* Darton, Longman & Todd, '85 p. 62.
6. *Prayer, The Transforming Friendship,* Lion, Oxford, '89 p. 48.

Chapter 9

1. *To Pray and to Love,* p. 8.
2. *Dynamics of Spiritual Life,* Paternoster Press, '79 pp. 383–84.
3. This is further developed in my book *Living Well,* HarperCollins, 1998, in the chapter entitled "Mind the Gap."

Chapter 10

1. *Be Still and Know,* Fount Paperbacks, London, '82 p. 27.
2. *The Lord's Prayer* (the prayer of integrated liberation), p. 10.
3. *The Man Who Wrestled with God,* p. 1.
4. *Thy Will Be Done (Praying the Our Father as Subversive Activity),* Orbis Books, Maryknoll, '77 p. 2.

Chapter 11

1. *Prayer,* p. 179.
2. *Still Following Christ in a Consumer Society,* Orbis Books, Maryknoll, '91 p. 3.
3. Ibid., p. 17.
4. *Collected Poems,* 1909–35, p. 157.

5. *Five for Sorrow, Ten for Joy,* Darton, Longman, & Todd, London, '85 p. 3.
6. *Families without Fatherhood,* IEA Health and Welfare Unit, London, '92 p. 66.

Chapter 12

1. *Be Still and Know,* Fount Paperbacks, London, '82 p. 12.
2. *Cycles of Affirmation,* Darton, Longman, & Todd, '75 p. 122.
3. *Christian Maturity,* IVF, Leicester, '64 p. 70.
4. *Prayer: Letters to Malcolm,* Fount, p. 91.
5. *God of Surprises,* p. 45.
6. *Prayer,* p. 125.

Postscript

1. *God of Surprises,* p. 22.
2. *Dynamics of Spiritual Life,* Paternoster Press, Exeter, '79 p. 160.
3. Ibid., p. 19.
4. *Blessings: Reflections on the Beatitudes,* p. 18.

Robert Warren is currently a Springboard missioner. Springboard is the evangelism initiative of the archbishops of Canterbury and York. Earlier, he spent twenty two years as the vicar, then Team Rector, of St. Thomas's, Crookes in Sheffield where he saw the church grow to over a thousand worshipers each Sunday.

For the next five years he was the National Officer for Evangelism of the General Synod Board of Mission, where he focused particularly on how the church can live and demonstrate the gospel in the context of our changing world. He took up his present post in November 1998.

He is the author of a number of books, including two on new ways of being church *(Building Missionary Congregations* [Church House Publishing] and *Being Human Being Church* [Marshall Pickering]). He is one of the five authors of the *Emmaus* initiation course now being used in over two thousand churches. Among his other writing is the Mid-term report on the Decade of Evangelism, *Signs of Life* (HarperCollins), in which he identifies a number of trends in the way that evangelism is taking place today. His latest book, *Living Well* (HarperCollins), is an exploration of the Beatitudes and their challenge to Christian living today.

Robert and his wife Ann now live in Ripon. His present work involves him in a wide travelling, speaking, and consultancy role throughout the United Kingdom and beyond. Robert and Ann have three grown-up daughters.